Pulping Fictions

Film/Fiction

The Film/Fiction series addresses the developing interface between English and Media studies, in particular the cross-fertilisation of methods and debates applied to analyses of literature, film and popular culture. Not only will this series capitalise upon growing links between departments of English and Media throughout Britain, it will also debate the consequences of the blurring of such disciplinary boundaries.

Editors
Deborah Cartmell – I.Q. Hunter – Heidi Kaye – Imelda Whelehan

Advisory Editor
Tim O'Sullivan

Film/Fiction volume 1

Pulping Fictions

Consuming Culture Across the Literature/Media Divide

Edited by
**Deborah Cartmell, I.Q. Hunter, Heidi Kaye
and Imelda Whelehan**

Pluto Press

LONDON • CHICAGO, IL.

First published 1996 by Pluto Press
345 Archway Road, London N6 5AA
and 1436 West Randolph,
Chicago, Illinois 60607, USA

British Library Cataloguing in Publication Data
A catalogue record for this book is available from the British
Library

ISBN 0 7453 1071 9 hbk

Library of Congress Cataloging in Publication Data
Pulping fictions: consuming culture across the English-media
    divide/edited by Deborah Cartmell ... [et al.].
        160p. 22cm. — (Film/fiction: v. 1)
        Includes bibliographical references and index.
        ISBN 0–7453–1071–0 (hbk.)
        1. Motion pictures and literature. I. Cartmell, Deborah.
    II. Series.
    PN1995.3.P85   1996
    791.43—dc20   95–52785
                                                            CIP

Printing history
03 02 01 00 99 98 97 96 8 7 6 5 4 3 2 1

Designed and produced for Pluto Press by
Chase Production Services, Chipping Norton, OX7 5QR
Typeset from disk by Stanford DTP Services, Milton Keynes
Printed in the EC by J.W. Arrowsmith, Bristol

Contents

Introduction – Pulping Fictions: Consuming Culture Across the Literature/Media Divide

Imelda Whelehan and Deborah Cartmell

'Pulp fiction' suggests trash and transitoriness: magazines and paperbacks, produced from poor-quality wood-pulp whose contents are formulaic and sensationalist. These fictions are designed for mass circulation and rapid turnover; they have a built-in obsolescence and will rapidly be 'pulped'. Quentin Tarantino offers us a dictionary definition of 'pulp fiction' in the epigraph to his movie of the same name, inviting us to consider the written word 'fiction' – along with its demise, 'pulp'. The title puts in a nutshell what can be perceived as popular cinema's threat to more 'worthy academic pursuits' (that is, the ultimate destruction of the book by the film). Similarly, horrified defenders of traditional English studies lament the fated take-over by media studies of English, with courses in *Star Trek* and *Batman* replacing those in Milton and Shakespeare.[1] There is no doubt that media studies will continue to seduce students away from more traditional subject areas (in Britain in 1995 there were approximately 1500 fewer English 'A'-level students than in the previous year, while media students increased by roughly the same number). English departments, with an eye to economic and academic survival, are increasingly joining up with media studies. In the light of current changes in the English curriculum, the volumes published in the *Film/Fiction* series aim to interrogate the interface between English and media studies by unashamedly admitting to and taking full advantage of consumer demand, and thereby examining the construction and consumption of the reader/viewer.[2]

1

Tarantino's dictionary definition tantalises us with the suggestion that popular cinema offers the viewer a similar range of sensations to that of mass market fiction. The marketing of such fiction capitalises on the growing consumer culture of the latter half of the twentieth century. Unlike highbrow fiction, which has tended to obscure the mechanisms of production which facilitate the journey of the great work from writer to reader, trash fiction monitors the tastes, identities and aspirations of its audience. In pulp fiction, the author is subordinated to genre. Yet Tarantino reasserts his authorship as a cult director, acclaimed as the postmodern *auteur* of increasingly self-reflexive and highly sophisticated intertextual cinema. In an ironic reversal of the conventional fiction to film adaptation, Tarantino's film scripts are becoming fictional classics – *Pulp Fiction* has become the bestselling film script ever. Far from being disposable moments on the postmodern screen, Tarantino's words are recited, repeated and committed to memory.[3]

Tarantino's work illustrates the changing relationships between production and consumption in the postmodern moment, where the high/lowbrow divide is increasingly destabilised. This volume of *Film/Fiction* debates the multitudinous ways in which such destabilisations are achieved, and ponders their implications for cultural studies today. In particular it looks at adaptations, whether they be the transformation of narrative from one textual site to another, or the translation of history and notions of the past into film. Despite the fact that the high/lowbrow divide is constantly collapsed in postmodern theory and in contemporary popular cultural practice, there is still a tendency – in both literary and media studies – to privilege the literary or the art-house movie over that which is consumed at a mass level. This cultural elitism is nowhere more apparent than in the adaptation of classic literature into commercial film, where the finished product tends to be judged against the impossible – its closeness to what the writer and/or reader 'had in mind'. To offset this, there is, of course, the 'novelisation', a growing development since the mid-1970s which, in Tarantino's case, retains a clear sense of its cinematic origins in the form of a film script.[4] A focus on film 'adaptations/interpretations' of classic literature allows us to scrutinise some continuing tensions in literary and film analyses, which betray an abiding hostility to mass culture and a reluctance to engage with a wider postmodern field of cultural production, where we 'have to think about thinking'.[5]

John O. Thompson, in the opening essay, tackles the unease with which film and TV adaptations are often greeted. This centres around the comparisons of the 'original' with its adaptation. The film has somehow not only to meet the demands of 'literariness' located in the original but also has to satisfy the economic and ideological requirements of its market. The disingenuous notion that superior adaptations successfully capture what the author 'had in mind' is also cleverly hijacked by *auteur*-directors such as Kenneth Branagh. As Deborah Cartmell and Heidi Kaye show in their respective discussions of Branagh's *Henry V* and *Mary Shelley's Frankenstein*, Branagh claims to restore to texts the authenticity debased in previous cinematic adaptations. Yet the process of re-novelisation (Branagh's screenwriters, for instance, 'novelised' *Mary Shelley's Frankenstein)* exploits the postmodern penchant for intertextuality (life, art, other films). He offers the audience an adaptation which is unashamedly late twentieth-century while ironically pandering to a popular desire that adaptations be faithful to the 'original'. Of course, as John O. Thompson points out, the film adaptation does not simply *concretise* an idea of the literary text, whether it be the idea of the writer, audience or director.

While Thompson uses the two screen versions of *The Vanishing* to allegorically pursue his view of adaptation forestalling the sense of 'loss' of the original, Ken Gelder takes up the notion of 'planning' in his analysis of the evolution of *Interview with the Vampire* on film. Gelder foregrounds the context in which the process of adaptation takes place – the 'field of production' (and the production of the 'field') of author/authority, bestsellers, commercial cinema, Hollywood stars and academics – whilst Bourdieu characterises the literary and artistic field as relatively autonomous from, but still affected by, the field of economic and political profit.[6]

Gelder shows that two contrasting positions for Anne Rice set up a tension within the cultural and economic fields. The film of the novel necessarily displaces the author; she is merely

one authority among many *auteurs*. Rice's responses to the
adaptation offer a third positioning of the author, shown by
Gelder's account of Anne Rice's unanticipated intervention in
the adaptation of *Interview with the Vampire*. Rice resists the
director Neil Jordan's realisation of the book on screen by
overwriting her own authority as the sole creator of the work,
and in particular the representations of the chief characters.
Rice wishes to assert her original intentions over wider
production considerations, and does so by denying her 'proper'
place in the restricted realm of the literary. The field of cultural
production turns out to offer a number of available positions,
a hierarchy of authorities where individuals can or cannot
choose to occupy the most appropriate space (e.g. Tom Cruise's
refusal to have an opinion about the finished film), or can be
appropriated 'out' of the field in a way which emphasises the
restrictiveness of the originary field.

Anne Rice's battle over the rights to the film of her novel
can be seen in the context of Virginia Woolf's view of the literary
text as the hapless victim of the predatory activities of a
masculine cinema. Woolf asserts that textual authenticity is
at stake, despite her observation that famous novels seem to
invite visual realisation. Acknowledging Woolf's concern about
possible tensions between narrative comprehension and visual
apprehension, Nicola Shaughnessy sees Sally Potter's adaptation
of *Orlando* as concerned with the exploitation of
textual/cinematic strategies rather than with any faithful
reproduction of character. It is a text, she argues, which might
be viewed as 'an offspring of its original'.[7]

While Shaughnessy pays tribute to the means by which
Sally Potter dramatises gender duality (not only in the representation of Orlando's shifting gender identities, but in the
casting of Jimmy Sommerville as gilded angel and Quentin Crisp
as Queen), Branagh attempts to redress gender imbalance in
his portrayal of motherhood and women's roles in *Mary
Shelley's Frankenstein* while, as Heidi Kaye argues, creating a film
which entrenches gender difference. The woman-positive
elements of Branagh's version depend upon an insertion of
Mary Shelley's 'life story' into the narrative, and in this way
Mary Shelley's Frankenstein becomes Kenneth Branagh's *Mary
Shelley's Frankenstein*.

In many ways Branagh's stamp of authority/authenticity on *Mary Shelley's Frankenstein* is prefigured in his screen adaptations of *Henry V* and *Much Ado About Nothing*. He is popularly seen as the director-genius who realises the 'truth' of a text as well as offering an accessible and enjoyable version of an otherwise stodgy classic. As Deborah Cartmell observes, in his adaptation of Shakespeare's *Henry V*, Branagh challenges Laurence Olivier's 1945 version of the same play, while activating relations between 'high' and 'popular' culture in order to attract the widest possible audience to Shakespeare. In the same way that *Mary Shelley's Frankenstein* is very '1990s' in its attempt to flesh out the female roles and, more suspiciously, its typically 'post-feminist' will to appropriate 'feminist' issues for anti-feminist purposes,[8] so Branagh's *Henry V*, with its confusion of anti-imperialist sentiment and nostalgia for a social and cultural stability, offers a Shakespeare for the late 1980s.

The BBC's dramatisation of George Eliot's *Middlemarch* is regarded as similarly a product of its time. Jenny Rice and Carol Saunders explore the consequences of the decision to film *Middlemarch* in Stamford. Just as commercial Hollywood literary tie-ins become the sum of their merchandise, so that it is impossible to determine where production ends and consumption begins, so 'Middlemarch'/Stamford democratises the entry into 'high' culture by offering access to a 'literary place' without demanding acquaintance with the originary text (or even its TV adaptation).

The next three papers in this volume raise issues about adaptation in different contexts, from Angela Carter's own adaptability in becoming her translator from fiction to film, to the transference of the grand narratives of history into theme park youth culture in *Bill & Ted's Excellent Adventure*, to the way Mel Brooks's 'irreverent' *Robin Hood: Men in Tights* ironically offers more fidelity to the folk tradition than the previous screen realisations it parodies. Postmodernism is after all seen to be 'full of jokes',[9] and it is always difficult to know whether the jokes are 'serious' or not. Catherine Neale detects a reluctance on the part of critics to identify contradictions in Angela Carter's work, which is explained in part by the weight and frequency of Carter's own self-reflexive commentaries. It is always possible, however, that the joke is on the critics themselves. Even after her death, Carter exerts her influence over her critical reception, though her integrity is tempered by a cool head for business. This is not so surprising, given Carter's postmodern disregard for generic and disciplinary boundaries, where the writer is critic, teacher, and scriptwriter – although Neale characterises Carter's two film adaptations as 'curiously downbeat hybrids'.[10] Carter's screenplays, Neale argues, bear the weight of their literary origins and, as a result, the images tend to appear archaic and risk being rendered comical.

Carter's adaptations depend upon the viewer's familiarity with her work – the literary text is thus both prerequisite for and superior to the film. Since the late 1980s, however, there has been a host of Hollywood films which depend not so much on a viewer's literary sophistication as their fluency with the gestures, signs and symbols of postmodern popular culture. In a sense, as I.Q. Hunter argues, these 'Dumb White Guy' films, as exemplified by *Bill & Ted's Excellent Adventure*, refer to nothing but their own generic forebears and mainstream popular culture. The jokes demand an encyclopedic familiarity with what would be considered 'debased' forms of knowledge. Bill and Ted, threatened with failing history, remake 'history' by exploiting the narrative possibilities offered by popular cinema and television. They travel through time selecting famous figures from the past to feature in their school presentation. This, in turn, is the basis for a (heavy metal) gig. Rather than Bill and Ted awakening to the pleasures of higher learning, their integration of such disparate characters as Socrates, Joan of Arc, Billy the Kid, Napoleon, Freud, Beethoven and Lincoln into the world of mall and leisure park teases the audience with a view of the contemporary US as an achieved utopia, with Bill and Ted as the future 'great ones'.[11] Bill and Ted, by summoning 'history' to San Dimas 1988, obliterate conventional views of progress and conflict, emptying the past of ideology. Their familiarity with history as it is recycled through films enables them to take an untroubled voyage through some great moments in order to appropriate them.

Robin Hood would not, of course, be out of place in Bill and Ted's excursion through (Hollywood) history (in fact the medieval sequence in *Bill & Ted* recalls the Errol Flynn *Adventures of Robin Hood*) and Stephen Knight selects Mel Brooks's *Robin Hood: Men in Tights* (1993) to scrutinise the dubious stamp of authenticity courted by some film versions and pilloried by Brooks. In the hierarchy of 'quality' film adaptations of the Robin Hood folk myth, Brooks's is popularly perceived as one of the trashiest. Its expansive and irreverent comic perspective negates the 'real' Robin Hood story only, as Knight argues, to reveal itself as a natural descendant of the Robin Hood tradition in which comic transgression and parody are central dynamics. In contrast to *Robin Hood: Prince of Thieves* (1991), which attempts to locate itself in an indeterminate authentic historical space, Brooks's version self-consciously exposes its own Hollywood genesis by means of playful metafictionality (when the cast refer to their scripts) and knowing intertextuality. As Knight demonstrates, the film achieves much of its dynamic from comically appropriating key scenes from other Robin Hood classics, eschewing the possibility of a 'serious' adaptation, and simultaneously exposing such attempts as mawkish and moralistic.

Knight is not arguing that Brooks produces the 'authentic' Robin Hood movie; rather that Brooks's version dramatises the tensions at work in the tradition 'so powerful that it encloses, as in any trickster-based genre, its own empowering element of trash and self-trashing'.[12] The comedy of Brooks and that found in *Bill & Ted* couples banality with a bravado which seduces the audience into suspecting that a more serious message might be secreted beneath the playful surface – a tension more apparent in *Pulp Fiction*.

In the final paper of this volume, Peter and Will Brooker foreground what they perceive as Quentin Tarantino's serious mission. Charges against Tarantino as exploiting the banal and vulgar tastes of mass culture are refuted in their reading of *Pulp Fiction*, in which the director is seen to redeem and recast 'the pulp of postmodernism' by embedding in the text narratives of re-invention and re-birth. The film's violent episodes (such as the plunging of the hypodermic needle into Mia Wallace) are by no means gratuitous, but illustrate Tarantino's overriding concern with the possibility of hope and renewal. According to Brooker and Brooker, Tarantino's censorious, high-minded critics are, in fact, provided with a 'worthy message' – the very thing they see as lacking in the productions of 'junk culture'. Conversely the more 'worthy' adaptations of the 'classics', such as those accomplished by Branagh, engender occasional bursts of laughter (how else can we respond when confronted with the vision of a giant scrotum?) in face of their alleged weightiness.

The film/fiction interface invites us to debate such ironies, and to insert them into our bank of contemporary cultural references which, as up-to-the-minute knowing academics and students, should be a heady melange of trash and the traditional. Necessarily, academic attention transforms the popular cultural production into something else, something which might gain value as cultural capital in its brush with scholarly attention. The commodification of the classics offers an interesting reversal of these possibilities, however, where a chain of references, local and immanent to the new adopted form, are generated and infinitely dispersed.

Notes

1. See for instance, Melanie Phillips, 'The videotic age of the Philistine', *Observer*, 13 August 1995, p. 25.
2. See David Morley, 'Theories of consumption in media studies', in David Miller (ed.), *Acknowledging Consumption*, (London: Routledge, 1995).
3. See Chris Petit's review of Tarantino's film script of *Natural Born Killers*, *Guardian*, 28 July 1995.
4. See John Sutherland, *Bestsellers* (London: Routledge and Kegan Paul, 1981), p. 32.
5. Angela McRobbie, *Postmodernism and Popular Culture* (London: Routledge, 1994), p. 8.
6. Pierre Bourdieu, *The Field of Cultural Production: Essays on Art and Literature,* trans. and ed. Randal Johnson (Oxford: Polity Press, 1993), pp. 36–7.
7. See Shaughnessy, this volume.
8. Heidi Kaye, this volume.
9. McRobbie, *Postmodernism and Popular Culture*, p. 3.
10. See Catherine Neale, this volume.
11. Although, as Hunter points out, the view of the future as entirely rock-oriented, with everyone playing air guitar and

adopting identical forms of greeting, might be regarded as rather chilling.
12. See Knight, this volume.

Further Reading

Bazin, Andre, *What Is Cinema?* (Berkeley: University of California Press, 1967).

Bennett, Tony, Graham Martin and Bernard Waites, *Popular Culture: Past and Present* (London: Routledge, 1981).

Bordwell, David, *Narration in the Fiction Film* (London: Routledge, 1986).

Bourdieu, Pierre, *The Field of Cultural Production: Essays on Art and Literature*, trans. and ed. Randal Johnson (Oxford: Polity Press, 1993).

Branagh, Kenneth, *Mary Shelley's Frankenstein: The Classic Tale of Terror Reborn on Film* (London: Ran, 1994).

Donald, James (ed.), *Fantasy and the Cinema* (London: BFI, 1989).

Eco, Umberto, *Travels in Hyperreality* (London: Picador, 1987).

Fukuyama, Francis, *The End of History and the Last Man* (Harmondsworth: Penguin, 1992).

Holderness, Graham, *Shakespeare Recycled: The Making of Historical Drama* (Brighton: Harvester, 1992).

Ingarden, Roman, *The Literary Work of Art*, trans. George G. Grobovicz (Evanston: Northwestern University Press, 1973).

Hirsch, E.D. Jr., *Cultural Literacy: What Every American Needs to Know* (Boston: Houghton Mifflin, 1987).

Kamps, Ivo (ed.), *Shakespeare Left and Right* (London: Routledge, 1991).

Lury, Celia, *Cultural Rights: Technology, Legality, and Personality* (London: Routledge, 1993).

Lyotard, Jean-Francois, *The Inhuman* (Oxford: Polity Press, 1991).

Mast, Gerald, Marshall Cohen and Leo Braudy, (eds), *Film Theory and Criticism: Introductory Readings* (Oxford: Oxford University Press, 1992).

McRobbie, Angela, *Postmodernism and Popular Culture* (London: Routledge, 1994).

Miller, David (ed.), *Acknowledging Consumption* (London: Routledge, 1995).

Postman, Neil, *Amusing Ourselves to Death: Public Discourse in the Age of Show Business* (New York: Viking, 1985).

O'Neill, John, *The Poverty of Postmodernism* (London: Routledge, 1994).

Reynolds, Peter (ed.), *Novel Images: Literature in Performance* (London: Routledge, 1993).

Sage, Lorna (ed.), *Flesh and the Mirror: Essays on the Art of Angela Carter* (London: Virago, 1994).

Said, Edward, *Culture and Imperialism* (London: Chatto & Windus, 1993).

Screen, The Sexual Subject: 'Screen' Reader in Sexuality (London: Routledge, 1992).

Sutherland, John, *Bestsellers* (London: Routledge & Kegan Paul, 1981).

Twitchell, James B., *Carnival Culture: The Trashing of Taste in America* (New York: Columbia University Press, 1992).

Zurbrugg, Nicholas, *The Parameters of Postmodernism* (London: Routledge, 1993).

1

'Vanishing' Worlds: Film Adaptation and the Mystery of the Original

John O. Thompson

The one sure thing about the topic 'literature and film' is that
it is not going to go away, however much it may seem like a
secondary distraction to the dedicated reader and the dedicated
viewer alike. 'Adaptation' has been from its earliest days one
of cinema's major activities. Before the cinema, and now con-
currently with it, adaptation has been a major activity of the
theatre as well; and now there is television. Nor should radio
and the *bande dessinée* be left out of account. And what of CD-
ROM and 'multi-media'? Something *wants* there to be a flow
of narrative and expository material from one form to another.

Despite this, the adaptation phenomenon has always made
people uneasy. In fact, there is quite a tangle of grounds for
unease, many of them unfashionable but not on that account
simply dismissable or without ongoing effects in our
spontaneous evaluation of the literature–film relationship. I
am thinking of considerations of 'authenticity' (the original
is authentic, the adaptation is a simulacrum), of 'fidelity' (the
adaptation is a deformation or dilution of the original), of art-
form 'specificity' (the literary original, if it is valuable, must
unfold its material in terms of distinctive literariness, and this
must be lost in a filmed version, while the filmed version
itself represents a lost opportunity to develop material of a
specifically filmic sort), and of 'massification' (the original must
be 'harder', more cognitively demanding, than the adaptation,
or the latter would not be the more popular form for a mass
audience; but then the easy access to the material must involve
deskilling the reader/viewer).

These concerns look unfashionable because, to put it quickly and roughly, they are pre-Derridean and pre-postmodern. For my purposes, the name 'Derrida' can here stand for a number of intricate demonstrations by himself and others that 'authenticity' is a deeply problematic concept; and the term 'postmodern' can stand for a number of challenges to the value hierarchisation involved in the modernist claim that painting is best when most painterly, literature when most writerly, and so on. The older positions stand convicted of being both dogmatic and elitist, as well as naive. Indeed, the phenomenon of adaptation looks precisely like a crucial case of what the older positions can't adequately handle.

Of course, you can, and no doubt should on occasion, make particular adverse judgements that parallel the general ones. A particular adaptation can be shown to betray its original, to take on material that doesn't work well in the new medium, or to be by comparison with the original stupid and stupidifying. (I even think, though this would be harder to establish, that some adaptations could be shown to be more simulacral, 'hollower' in some way, than others.) Thus, I happen not to think much of the filmed version of *The Silence of the Lambs*, and some of my arguments for that judgement would no doubt run along the above-mentioned lines. But it is positively to my argumentative advantage to keep such complaints particular to the case at hand rather than to have them cover adaptation generically.

Nevertheless, I do think there is *something* generically eerie about adaptation, and consequently about the film–literature relationship insofar as this is very largely to do with adaptation. My hope in this essay is to make some progress at specifying wherein the eeriness actually lies.

Something wants there to be a flow of narrative and expository material from one form to another: what? One important, truly general answer to this question is: the market. This has always been the case, throughout the history of the cinema within a historical era which is that of the commodity; it is now even more markedly the case, as the logic of the market and of the media commodity shifts into satellite, cable, 'electronic superhighway' mode, with its ever-increasing need for 'product'.

Why should the market favour adaptation? And what does the fact that the market favours adaptation lead us to think about adaptation? What do we think of the market, in this field? I set out these questions only to set them aside for now, because I want to examine *something else* which wants there to be adaptation, something which it is harder to name.

Harriett Hawkins has discussed *Gone With the Wind* in a manner which illuminatingly brings out the will-to-adaptation as a function of readers' desires. She focuses on its producer-*auteur* David O. Selznick's insistence on a certain sort of fidelity in the adaptation:

> Audiences, he felt, understood the conventions of the cinema and were prepared to forgive necessary cuts and omissions, but they did not like gratuitous alterations to familiar scenes and characters. In his productions of *Gone With the Wind* and *Rebecca* … alike he adamantly vetoed changes to the original characterization and construction on the grounds that no one, not even the author, could be certain why a play or novel had caught the fancy of the public. 'If there are faults in construction', he told the journalist Bosley Crowther, 'it is better to keep them than to try to change them around because no one can certainly pick out the chemicals which contribute to the makings of a classic. And there is always the danger that by tampering you may destroy the essential chemical.'[1]

Would that this modest pragmatism were more widely shared! Hawkins continues:

> From his first reading of *Gone With the Wind*, Selznick realized that, in visual details, dialogue, costuming and characteriz-ation, Margaret Mitchell had imagined a great movie. He therefore wanted the film to seem like an exact photographic reproduction of the book, including 'every well-remembered scene' either in 'faithful transcription of the original or in keeping with the spirit of Miss Mitchell's book'.[2]

It is at this point that the detail of what Selznick and Hawkins are saying gets surprising. For what would 'imagining a great movie' be like as a by-product of writing a novel? And, even more puzzlingly, what could 'an exact photographic reproduction of the book' be? If I held up a photograph of a copy of Mitchell's book, I would be presenting you with 'an exact photographic representation of the book', but this is clearly not what is meant! What is to be 'exactly photographed' is what Mitchell has imagined. But how is 'the imagined', ideational as it is by definition, to be photographed (mechanically reproduced, from a material original)?

Hawkins quotes Richard Corliss's review of one of the last decade's quintessential examples of widely disliked adaptation, the Brian De Palma-directed film of Tom Wolfe's *The Bonfire of the Vanities*:

> 'Novel readers are a possessive lot' because they 'have already made their own imaginary film version of the book – cast it, dressed the sets, directed the camera'. In many cases, so have the novelists themselves: De Palma's film flopped because 'Tom Wolfe had already created a great movie in the minds of his readers'.[3]

Have we one or two or 'n' number of 'movies in minds' here: the one created by Margaret Mitchell or Tom Wolfe, simply by writing something to be read; the one(s) created in readers' minds as they read? Is writing already proto-adaptation? Is reading already quasi-adaptation?

Something that wants there to be adaptations is at the least a readerly desire, now quite possibly linked to the writer's desire, to compare his or her 'virtual movie' of the original, prepared (more or less sketchily) during the reading process because we now read as movie-goers or television viewers, to an actual moving image experience. We compare *the* movie to *our* 'movie', which is in our view the author's 'movie' (we readers are such faithful adaptors!), and praise or blame, forgive or condemn, as we see fit.

How should we name or characterise the force which is at work here? The aesthetic phenomenology of Roman Ingarden distinguishes between the literary work of art in itself, 'a very complex structured object', and 'the mode of appearance of the work, the concrete form in which the work itself is apprehended'.[4] One work, many *concretisations*, is how Ingarden puts it.

> The complexity of a total apprehension of a work is such that the experiencing ego has too much to do at once, as it were, and thus cannot give itself equally to all the components ... [T]he literary work is never *fully* grasped in *all* its strata and components but always only partially, always, so to speak, in only a *perspectival foreshortening*.[5]

This perspectival giving of itself by the work is in turn to be distinguished from the *merely* particular, subjective, idiosyncratic experiences had by each reader in reading.

All this quickly gets very philosophically intricate, of course, and it is notable how keen Ingarden, like Husserl before him, is to fend off any 'subjectivist' account of experience in general and aesthetic experience in particular. However, I would argue that 'concretisation' is a useful term for both *Gone With the Wind* as concretely appearing to its readers and for a 'something' that can consequently be filmed, be photographically 'captured' or rendered, in much the same way as physical objects (themselves never experienceable fully and outside of 'perspective', of course) can be photographically captured. Adaptation would then take place because there is a *drive to concretise*, inseparable from the very experience of an 'original', and the adaptation is a way in which a certain materialisation of the concretisation is, or is hoped to be, achieved.

Extending Ingarden's insight beyond the literary, I see no reason not to speak of a comparable distinction between the filmic work of art and its concretisations by individual, more or less attentive, spectators on particular occasions. Indeed, 'fidelity' comparisons are best thought of as comparisons between a concretion in one medium and one in another; this would help to account for why one person's shocking infidelity is another's insignificant variation.[6] If, after you read the novel, a very specific 'vision' of Scarlett O'Hara had been central to your pre-film concretisation of *Gone With the Wind*, you might have found Vivien Leigh 'not right for the part'; but if, to use another Ingarden term, your sense of Scarlett had included a fair amount of 'indeterminacy',[7] it is likely that you would not have found the Leigh casting a problem. Hawkins has some historical data on this:

> [F]emale readers polled by fan magazines did not strongly support any particular star for the part. They saw Scarlett in the mind's eye as described by Margaret Mitchell – green-eyed, dark-haired, with a tiny waist – and otherwise imaginatively and emotionally projected themselves into the role. By contrast, Clark Gable was the public's overwhelming favourite for Rhett.[8]

Hawkins also points out the possibility of determination retrospectively donated from the later concretisation to the earlier:

> [I]f countless admirers of the original novel agreed that green-eyed Vivien Leigh acted just like Scarlett as described by Margaret Mitchell ('She is my Scarlett!' Mitchell is often quoted as saying at the première), innumerable later readers have seen Scarlett O'Hara as looking, dressing and acting just like Leigh did in the film.[9]

A concretisation is an idea (or a set of linked ideas). I want now, as a final bit of conceptual groundwork for this essay's purposes, to contrast concretisations with *plans*, which I take to be equally 'ideational'. I concretise on the basis of semiotic material presented to me by the work of art, which I encounter in the present as a complex object created in the past (or, in the case of improvisation, simultaneously to my reception). I plan in the present to achieve in the future a planned-for outcome.

The role of planning in the achievement of the 'original' work of art varies case by case, project by project (with Edgar Allan Poe a notable, and notably devious, early rhetorical advocate of the ultra-planned work). There is undoubtedly an aesthetic of the unplanned, of the aleatory, of the impossible-to-anticipate, and many of the cinema's most exquisite moments participate in that aesthetic. But planning is *of the essence* of adaptation, if we think of it in Ingardenian terms, because to photograph a concretisation, or more broadly 'what the author has imagined' / 'what the reader has imagined', involves a complicated, resource-hungry deployment of material objects, equipment and performers in order to 'materialise' these ideations. And such deployment is impossible without detailed planning.

'Margaret Mitchell had imagined a great movie.' This sentence is deeply puzzling, which is not to say that it is nonsensical or badly expressed. But it is, at the least, elliptical. An unpacking of it might run something like this: 'Margaret Mitchell, in creating the verbal text *Gone With the Wind*, however she did it (and doing it will have involved mental operations of a diverse sort, including some planning), brought into being a text whose concretisations were to turn out to be photographable to excellent effect.' But concretisations as such are not photographable, so the unpacking must continue: 'whose concretisations could, with further planning, be physically embodied in order to be photographed to excellent effect'.

It is all very well for Corliss's readers of *The Bonfire of the Vanities* to 'have already made their own imaginary film version of the book – cast it, dressed the sets, directed the camera': in being only an *imaginary* film version, the readers not being skilled professionals employed in the industry, the reader's version is not a work of planning, of preparing for the deployment of material resources to a desired end, namely, the achievement of a satisfactory second concretisation. It is, instead, primary concretisation, albeit conducted in a cultural context in which experience of the cinema importantly influences how readers concretise novels.

So much for a theoretical framework; for the remainder of this essay, I propose to explore further concretisation and its relations to planning and to viewing, but in less strictly conceptual terms. The various versions of a Dutch narrative will turn out to render some of these relations in the form of fiction, indeed of horror fiction.

The case of the double filmic adaptation of *The Vanishing*, whereby the same director, George Sluizer, made first a European version and then an American version of Tim Krabbe's short novel *Het Gouden Ei* / *The Golden Egg*, is a piquant one – and no less so for having generated what has been seen as a clear quality distinction: the European *Vanishing* has been well-received, the American *Vanishing* has been deplored. This only confirms a broader stereotype about the European art-house film, whereby we would expect the European *Vanishing* to be more faithful to its original, less commercial, more oblique hence more intelligent (presupposing a more cognitively active audience not needing things to be 'spelt out'), less 'sensational', than the American *Vanishing* – because, to put it bluntly, European film audiences are more cultured than American film audiences. On this account, what wanted *The Golden Egg* to be filmed in Europe was primarily the intrinsic concretisation potential of its own material; while what wanted *The Vanishing* (having thereby come into being perfectly satisfactorily) to be re-made in the US was simply, and stupidifyingly, the market.

My own view is that matters are not that straightforward (or that dull!). I should acknowledge at once that, yes, something has gone seriously askew in the American *Vanishing*, taken as a self-standing text: I can't see how any viewer possessing the cultural capital to view both *Vanishing*s comprehendingly could end up preferring the American one as an aesthetic object. However, you could say the same thing about Milton's *Paradise Regained* relative to *Paradise Lost* while still finding the later poem to be of great interest, not least as a sort of rejoinder to the earlier epic; and I do find in the American *Vanishing* a degree of 'rejoinder' quality, despite the film's overall unachieved feel.

If I am not so completely dismissive as most critics of the later *Vanishing*, I also found myself initially not so straight-forwardly persuaded by the earlier version as many critics have been, nor indeed by Krabbe's novel (insofar as I have made contact with it via the English translation by Claire Nicolas White). At least, I felt there to be a puzzle as to what the 'point' of the story is. But it turns out, I think, that what particularly puzzled me about the material has a curious relevance to some of the key issues surrounding adaptation.

Rex Hofman; Raymond Lemorne with his wife Simone (left nameless in the original novel) and daughters Denise and Gabrielle; Saskia Wagter (originally Ehlvest); Lienexe (originally Lieneke): these are the chief inhabitants of the *Vanishing* world.[10] What 'happens' is that Raymond murders Saskia and, some years later (eight, the novel says), murders Rex; in both cases, he commits 'the perfect crime'. Rex and Saskia suffer identical modes of death: each is buried alive.

The point of Saskia's death is that it has no point: Raymond has formed a plan for carrying through a perfect crime, and any ('respectable') woman whom he could lure into his car could have been the victim. To this degree, the death of Rex, as the death of the arbitrary victim's partner, is equally arbitrary, though Rex has also 'brought it upon himself' by carrying on the search for Saskia and then by agreeing to be drugged in order to find out from Raymond what exactly happened.

Now, what is the point of telling us this unpleasant tale? How does it instruct? How does it please? For the jacket note for the British video release of *The Vanishing*, Sluizer wrote:

> One thing that attracted me [to the novel] was that Tim didn't come up with all those standard psychological explanations for the kidnapper's behaviour, such as 'His mother beat him when he was a boy and therefore ... ' all of which I think is not interesting – there was nothing of that. Similarly, with my films every person is totally free to think whatever he wants, and interpret them as they [sic] wish. I simply provide a blueprint for audiences – I just give them the possibility to think. I know that I once said that people should be 'disturbed' by *The Vanishing*, but in fact I would like people to reflect on what they see ... [Unlike in gory 'films with cut throats',] with *The Vanishing*, it's the mental fear, to do with the fact that you recognise in the people something which you recognise in yourself, and which you don't want to accept.

The horror genre depends on the viewer's delight in being disturbed – a mysterious sort of delight, which for the purposes of this essay we can afford to leave unanalysed. What Sluizer suggests is that the particular disturbing delight on offer here is such as to gain from the lack of 'standard psychological explanation'. I suspect it also gains from other standard features of crime fiction being suppressed, notably any ethical meaning of a straightforward sort attaching to the deaths (the point is not that these innocent deaths are 'redeemed' via the punishment of the killer, nor even – though this might be more arguable – that Saskia's and then Rex's own deaths are somehow Rex's fault).

Delight, here, is globally provided by a cool, 'grown-up' capacity to enjoy narrative from which some of the standard devices for providing enjoyment have been removed. The instruction that can be derived immediately from this delight could be stated thus: do not expect life to be be fair, kind and meaningful; do not expect instruction. And in turn this is, while standard enough as an 'absurdist' message, itself disturbing enough to feed back into the horror delight.

However, this characterisation of the material is so far rather too simply 'subtractive'. It leaves out of account what positive elements of the material fascinate reader and viewer. Positively, the excitement of this material surely depends on the inter-section of two narrative lines whose difference from one another is maximised. Each has its 'core feel'. At the core of the Rex story is the pain of losing someone and not knowing what happened. This is something to which, I take it, we can all relate. At the core of the Raymond story, contrastively, is the pleasure of forming a plan, developing it and carrying it successfully through. And this too is something to which, I take it, we can all relate.

What renders this pain and this pleasure, within the *Vanishing* material, charged more strongly than merely everyday experience is that, on the loss side, the protagonist manages to suffer not once but twice (initial loss and then 'self-loss' in the pursuance of the quest for the lost or for the truth of the loss), while on the planning side, the protagonist plans something very bad and does so as part of a series of *actes gratuits* of an intriguing sort (self-injury, selfless good action, 'selfless' while monstrously selfish evil action).[11] Although I have said that the point is for the two narrative lines to feel wholly distinct, one could suggest a formula for their distinctness which would also capture a certain relatedness: on the one side, utter failure of reparation; on the other side, unqualified success in preparation.

The allegory of adaptation here (and remember, we have at least George Sluizer's permission to read his film as we will: 'every person is totally free to think what he wants') would translate thus: for Saskia and her death, read 'the original and its adaptive betrayal'; for Raymond and his plan, read 'the artist and his or her plan'; for Rex, his loss and his quest, read 'the reader/viewer and his or her curiosity'.

Saskia is, within the world of *The Vanishing*, both real and unplanned. 'Unplanning' hangs as an atmosphere over her and Rex (to the degree that his loss of her registers analogically as a kind of carelessness, powerfully embodied in the film in the scene where Rex's carelessness over petrol causes the car to stop dangerously in the tunnel, even though her vanishing turns out *not* to be the result of anyone's carelessness – quite the contrary). Her difficulty with French in her conversation with Raymond also places her in the unplanned, 'spontaneous/ sloppy' realm.

Once she is gone, Rex wants two 'readerly' things. He *wants her back*, he wants there to 'be' her (again) – just as the reader wants the adaptation to bring back the concretisation which was the reading experience. And he *wants to know what happened*, which is more readerly-in-the-first-instance: the reader always wants to know what happens. If Rex's continuing search for Saskia is registered as obsessive, especially in the light of the material's insistence that 'there are after all other women' (this is the whole point of the Lienexe/Lieneke figure in both film and novel),[12] so is the pre-postmodernist reader's search for the 'authentic' in adaptation. But the fatal attraction for Rex is the second: he *has to know* – and in some detail. (It is made very clear that Raymond lets him know that Saskia is dead before Rex accepts the drugged coffee; it is the investigation into the precise 'how' of that death that he pursues to the end.) Now to say here that Rex represents the reader in this regard does not seem to me very far-fetched. We, the reader/viewer, could have a less unhappy *Vanishing* ending very simply: Rex, faced with the bargain proposed, makes the other decision, and walks away from Raymond, to mourn, pick up his life, try to achieve revenge or justice, etc. How flat! *We* want to know; in a way, we thereby become as 'guilty' of Rex's death, and in much the same way, as he sometimes feels himself to have been of Saskia's, in the 'mind game' he speaks of to Lieneke: 'You can play all kinds of mind games. For instance, I am told that she is alive somewhere and perfectly happy. And I'm given a choice. She goes on living like that, or I get to know everything and she dies. Then I let her die.'[13]

Raymond, on the other hand, wants there to be something in preparation, something that would have the status, even if not 'gone through with', of the perfectly executable. What makes his plan so like that of the writer or of the film-maker in general is, precisely, what makes it in the particular writing and filming of this fiction so gripping. Everyone who admires the film singles out for praise Bernard-Pierre Donnadieu's embodiment of Raymond. It is as if this is both the most 'realised' figure in the novel and the most faithfully and resourcefully re-realised, concretised figure in the film because he is *the figure of realisation itself*: he brilliantly sets up an event, perfectly indifferent to the particular being of the person who will suffer through the event the liquidation of that being. This is scary but it is also, in these calculating times, these 'technological' times in the full Heideggerian sense, 'normal'. She, any she who will yield to the process, is there to hand, waiting to be murdered, as any 'original' is there to hand waiting to be adapted.

In the American version of *The Vanishing*, moment-by-moment details are retained in re-setting the material in the US, but, as Sluizer himself says, 'the events are similar but the soul is different'.[14] The obvious point that has been made about the American *Vanishing* is that it has a 'happy ending'. This is not even straightforwardly true (the Saskia equivalent after all remains dead), and is anyway not the key variation on the original material. What has importantly happened in the American version is that the figure of the new girl in our hero's life (Lienexe/Lieneke turned into Rita Baker, working-class heroine) becomes central: she emerges as a version of a generic figure from the last two decades' horror production who has been named by Carol Clover as the Final Girl,[15] the gutsy female survivor (final in a chain of women victims) of the terror unleashed by/constituting the plot.

The reader-equivalent figure is rescued by someone who has been marginal in earlier versions. The writer/director-equivalent figure is vanquished similarly. Who is this new force, allegorically? Common sense might say that the American *Vanishing* fails simply because a balance maintained in Krabbe's novel and Sluizer's first film had been liquidated in the course of crass commercial script development, and that was that. But the Final Girl solution is not intrinsically so dismissable, whatever the verdict on its successful carrying-through in the event might be.

Rita Baker, Final Girl, effectively says to the person with the plan, 'We've got your number, desist! die!' She effectively says to the 'entombed' reader/viewer: 'Relax, don't get obsessed, pay attention to me the living one rather than to her the dead one. I can handle it. You *know* now, beneath the earth, but I am above the earth *for* you and can rescue you (modestly allowing you a moment later to rescue me).'

I think the Final Girl here is, allegorically, the producer. She has the appropriate fidelity, analogous to the fidelity we saw Selznick speaking for; the appropriate 'can-do' mentality; and, crucially, the appropriate suspicion of the director's *auteur*-y planniness (she has plans of her own!). But if she is producer, shouldn't what all that involves, corporately, in terms of power, itself be registered? Over and above certain particular production miscalculations which the American *Vanishing* was patently a victim of, an allegorical reading would leave this Final Girl's underdog isolation, in the narrative, looking seriously phony. And so indeed, as it happens, it does look.

To retrace some steps here: I have proposed using the material of *The Vanishing* to think about adaptation. *The Vanishing* is a tale of mystery and imagination, to evoke Edgar Allan Poe again, who was himself so fascinated by the theme of premature burial. Adaptation, it would follow if one can 'figure' it by *The Vanishing*, is an affair, perhaps a dark affair, of mystery and imagination. Through the imaginative activity of planning, and all the consequent deployment of the material resources of the adaptive medium, the adaptation puts before the viewer a photographed version of what he or she has imaginatively but 'passively' (not executively) concretised in the reading process. (Of course, 'passivity' is not the right concept here: we need another, possibly Lyotard's 'passibility', the quiet, alert openness to the sensations evoked by the aesthetic object, on the threat to which by the market-technology complex he dubs 'Development', with its obsessive need to plan, he has written so eloquently.)[16] Evidently, this interplay of concretisation and planning is given a particularly grim treatment in the tale of Rex and Raymond: concretisation as loss, planning as demonic. Happier fictions could be used to think about these matters: why not? But horror has its claims as well.

I would expect my casting of Raymond as the planner would carry more immediate conviction than my casting of Saskia as the work and Rex as the reader. Let me conclude with a reflection on concretisation which returns us to the question 'What wants there to be adaptation?', now in an appropriately loss-oriented mode.

Here is a sad thought: there are books which, whether we were to die next week or fifty years from now, we will never get around to re-reading. We have, in enjoying them, perhaps intensely, already concretised them once or more than once, but what we have of them currently is only the memory of that. They do not strike us as vanished, dead, prematurely buried; they are there on our shelves, awaiting us. Still, death will come before we take up the chance to re-concretise them. (The situation regarding films used to be even more contingent, but the above holds word for word for the video collection.)

Something that wants there to be adaptation is this: the adaptation would reassure us, via the logic of photographic 'ontology' that Andre Bazin so notably explored,[17] that a concretisation has been photographed and thus saved from death. The 'successful' adaptation, from this viewpoint, provides us with a new concretion experience close enough to our initial concretion to pass muster as its photograph.

But, alas and of course, the very vehicle of reassurance, subject to the same mortality-based limitation, is no less already lost. There are photographs 'saving' the people and things I have lost which I will not get around to looking at again – so saving nothing, at least for me.[18]

Notes

1. Harriet Hawkins, 'Shared dreams: reproducing *Gone With the Wind*', in Peter Reynolds (ed.), *Novel Images: Literature*

in Performance (London: Routledge, 1993), pp. 122–38; Roland Flamini, *Scarlett, Rhett and a Cast of Thousands: The Filming of 'Gone With the Wind'* (London: Macmillan, 1978), p. 199.

2. Hawkins 'Shared dreams', p. 125, quoting from 'the producer's statement in the souvenir programme issued at the première of the film'.

3. Ibid., p. 124; Richard Corliss in *Time*, 1 April 1991, p. 72.

4. Roman Ingarden, *The Literary Work of Art* (Evanston: Northwestern University Press, 1973) p. 332. This is a translation by George G. Grabowicz of the third German edition of Ingarden's work (1965); the work first appeared as *Das literarische Kunstwerk* in 1931.

5. Ingarden, *The Literary Work of Art* , pp. 333–4 (Ingarden's emphasis).

6. Ingarden's more detailed explanation for the 'partiality' of the concretisation may be of help here. He writes: 'Of the entire manifold of simultaneously experienced (or executed) and interwoven acts and other experiences only a few are effected as central and with full activity by the ego; the rest, though still experienced and effected, are only "coeffected", coexperienced … Consequently, the parts and strata of the work being read that can be seen clearly are always different; the rest sink into a semi-darkness, a semivagueness, where they only covibrate and cospeak, and, precisely because of this, they colour the totality of the work in a particular manner' (ibid., pp. 333–4).

7. Cf. Ingarden, ibid., pp. 249–50. The English translation of Ingarden often uses the more vivid phrase 'spots of inde-terminacy'. 'If, e.g., a story begins with the sentence: "An old man was sitting at a table," etc., it is clear that the represented "table" is indeed a "table" and not, for example, a "chair"' but whether it is made of wood or iron, is four-legged or three-legged, etc., is left quite unsaid and therefore – this being a purely intentional object – *not determined* … Thus, in the given object, its qualification is *totally absent*: there is an "empty" spot here, a "spot of indeterminacy". As we have said, such empty spots are

impossible in the case of a real object. At most, the material may, for example, be unknown' (Ingarden's emphasis).

8. Hawkins, 'Shared dreams', p. 126.

9. Ibid. While the photographed Vivien Leigh is a 'real object' and therefore replete with determinations, so to speak, the application of a thoroughgoing 'Leigh visualisation' to the entire reading experience of a long novel strikes me as unlikely to be consistently carried through by a reader; but whether it is or isn't would seem more a question of subjective readerly experience than of Ingardenian concretisation as such.

10. In the American version, respectively: Jeff *Harriman*; Barney Cousins with his wife Helene and (only one) daughter *Denise*; Diane Shaver; Rita Baker. I can find no overlaps in the names save for the bits that I've italicised.

11. Raymond as a youth, sitting on a window-sill, wonders what would happen if he exercised the 'absurd' choice of deliberately falling, and does so. As a family man, he leaps into the water to save a potentially drowning child. Then he plans the crime. It is worth noting that the first two *actes gratuites* are virtually spontaneous; only the third, the crime, moves him into 'planning mode' (and of an exaggerated kind) while the spontaneity, the chance aspect of the choice of the *victim* remains absolute.

12. The crucial difference in the American *Vanishing* is that Rex's ultimate indifference to the representative 'life-goes-on' other women in his life (the novel stresses the plurality of women 'on tap' for the attractive Rex more than the first film does) is transformed into a deeply involved if troubled relationship with a 'successor partner' who both saves him and wins him. This moves the American *Vanishing* into terrain which is not unrelated to that of the Du Maurier and then Selznick/Hitchcock *Rebecca* – another film whose potential as an allegory of adaptation might reward exploration. I should acknowledge here the work of Lucy Richer, a student on the British Film Institute/Birkbeck College, University of London MA in Cinema and Television, whose MA dissertation (1993) on the film adaptations of *Rebecca* and

Orlando has greatly helped me focus on the adaptation issue.

13. Tim Krabbe, *The Vanishing*, (New York: Random House, 1993), p. 42.

14. Richard Kohl, 'The lady vanishes', *Time Out Amsterdam*, October 1993, pp. 10–11.

15. See Carol C. Clover, 'Her body, himself: gender in the slasher film', in James Donald (ed.), *Fantasy and the Cinema* (London: BFI, 1989), pp. 91–133 (originally in *Representations* 20 [1987]). Clover's argument is extended in her *Men, Women and Chainsaws* (London: BFI, 1992).

16. Jean-François Lyotard, *The Inhuman* (Oxford: Polity Press, 1991). 'Passibility as the possibility of experiencing (*pathos*) presupposes a donation. If we are in a state of passibility, it's that something is happening to us, and when this passibility has a fundamental status, the donation itself is something fundamental, originary. What happens to us is not at all something we have first controlled, programmed, grasped by a concept [*Begriff*]. Or else, if what we are passible to has first been plotted conceptually, how can it *seize us*?' (pp. 110–11). See also the crucial paragraph on pp. 116–17: 'About the confusion between passible and passive ... [Once,] when you painted, you did not ask for "interventions" from the one who looked, you claimed there was a community. The aim nowadays is not that sentimentality you still find in the slightest sketch by a Cézanne or a Degas, it is rather that the one who receives should not receive, it is that s/he does not let him/herself be put out ... let him/her reconstitute himself immediately and identify himself or herself as someone who intervenes. What we live by and judge by is exactly this will to action ... [This] implies the retreat of the passibility by which alone we are fit to receive and, as a result, to modify and do, and perhaps even to enjoy.'

17. André Bazin, 'The ontology of the photographic image', in *What Is Cinema?*, vol. 1 (Berkeley: University of California Press, 1967), pp. 9–16. Another Bazinian text in the same collection which is highly pertinent to the concerns of this paper is 'In defense of mixed cinema', pp. 53–75.

18. The uses of still photography within both the film versions of *The Vanishing* would sustain analysis. For instance, contrast the photographic reminder to Raymond of his first *acte gratuite*, which gives him the idea of looking vulnerable by (re)placing his arm in a sling (photography as aid to planning), with the ultra-Bazinian, and quite useless, photo of Saskia which is Rex's final visual record of her. A hidden photographic 'shrine', along with a disguised computer file (what would Bazin have made of computer files?) brings home to Rita, very painfully, Jeff's continuing obsession with the lost Diane. And what vanishes last in the original *Vanishing* are Saskia's and Rex's photographic images, first appearing in a newspaper account of the mysterious doubling of the one disappearance by the other, then visually held while the newspaper text disappears, in simple oval (old-fashioned portrait? *egg*?) framing. A more daring critical move would be to see Rex's death as a 'hyper-photograph' of Saskia's death (with Raymond as the 'camera'). Bazin's argument about photography as the technological fulfilment of the ambition behind mummification or the modelling of death-masks would then find here an appropriately macabre extension.

2

The Vampire Writes Back: Anne Rice and the (Re)Turn of the Author in the Field of Cultural Production

Ken Gelder

This chapter will look at the fortunes of a particular author in relation to the filming of one of her novels: Anne Rice's *Interview with the Vampire* (1975; released as a film at the end of 1994). I want to use Anne Rice as a case study, to look at how the author might function in relation to what can be called – following Pierre Bourdieu – 'the field of cultural production', a phrase which is suitably non-specific since what is involved here is not just the relationship between novelist and film, but also media which negotiate that relationship and which themselves constitute and produce that 'field'. My suggestion here is that, following the traumatic announcement by Roland Barthes of the 'death of the author' in the late 1960s, nevertheless the author is still *not quite* dead. Indeed, the author – and the image is obviously appropriate for an author of vampire novels in particular – may well be 'undead' in the sense that she may be able to be reanimated when her work is reproduced elsewhere in the field of cultural production. The notion of the 'death of the author' has two kinds of uses: firstly, it refers to the author's disappearance in the very act of writing, which enables often indeterminate meanings beyond the intentions of the author; and secondly (although this owes more to Walter Benjamin than Roland Barthes), it refers to the author's disappearance at the moment of 'mechanical reproduction' (e.g. through the film-of-the-novel), where the author's intentions may be only one contributing factor amongst many others. But during the filming of *Interview with the Vampire*, Anne Rice did *not* disappear. She returned to the scene of reproduction – and this is why I've broken this word in two in my title – by throwing a *turn*, a tantrum. She made the film an occasion for the author of the novel-on-which-it-was-based to 'have a turn', in both senses of that phrase. And in this way, she hasn't exactly *re*turned – but she hasn't exactly disappeared, either. By 'writing back' to the film of her novel, she unsettled the equilibrium of the field; she effected this primarily by becoming an author who did not behave like an author, an author who did not know her place (in the field of cultural production).

I have found Pierre Bourdieu's book, *The Field of Cultural Production* (1993), useful for this essay because it helps to organise our sense of how cultural production – and reproduction – operates. In relation to the artist – the author – the cultural field is structured by what he calls 'the distribution of available positions'.[1] The field gains its dynamics through 'position-takings' – one artist may take a position in relation to positions already occupied by artists he or she may wish to be identified with, or distinguished from, and so on. The point is, however, that this is not so much a struggle between or amongst artists-as-individuals, as a struggle built around those 'available positions', and the 'orientation of practice' an artist adopts in relation to them.[2] One chooses to become a popular novelist, for example; but even here, one can occupy an 'available position' in relation to conceptions of popularity (which is not a homogeneous thing) – conceptions which are *already* available in that field. Those available positions have values attached to them; they are located in culture in a certain way; and they locate the artist in a certain way, attributing to the artist certain effects in culture.

These available positions are often seen as variants on a binary opposition which can be expressed simply in terms of the difference between producing cultural goods for money (economic capital) and producing cultural goods for a less tangible kind of prestige (symbolic capital). This kind of difference is often invoked when we think about films on the one hand, and writing on the other: films, obviously, are a form of 'large-scale' production, while writing (novels, poetry in particular) is a form of 'restricted' production. Our conception of the 'author' is generally tied to this latter form: large-scale production, on the other hand, seems to do away with this concept. (Howard Becker's influential book *Art Worlds* [1982] is precisely about how social *groups* produce film; it describes how the intentions of an individual count for very little in the large-scale, incorporated world of film production.) But in fact, the relationship between large-scale production and restricted production is often unclear, especially in the realm of popular writing. The novelist Fay Weldon has given what seems like a belated account of the modern writer, when she claimed not long ago. 'The writer, like the scientist, is no longer pure. He/she works and creates, ultimately, for the profit of others. The scientist has to please the funding body; the writer, increasingly, has the publisher and script editor to please, else his/her work does not see the light of day.'[3] In the realm of the 'popular' in particular, this account has probably always been true – although it is worth thinking about why it is under renewal today (following middlebrow author Martin Amis's contract with HarperCollins for half-a-million pounds – to write a novel precisely about the writer's 'available positions' in relation to popular fiction – we can think of Amis himself as a highly constrained novelist in this respect, with only a limited number of available positions, partly because of his own genealogy).

Even a popular novelist can be 'returned' to the field of restricted production, however. After the release of the film of *Interview with the Vampire,* John Ezard wrote an article for The *Guardian* which took us back to the novel-upon-which-it-was-based, characterising that novel – even though it had sold over four million copies – as a text with a limited circulation:

> I spent, or misspent, part of the seventies trying to find someone to talk to about a story called *Interview With The Vampire*. I chanced on a copy 17 years ago in the small paperback section of a now long-shut Co-op furniture shop. The blurb said it was 'the most seductive evocation of evil ever written ... a strikingly original work of the imagination.'
>
> For once a blurb turned out to be right. Nothing since has shaken my belief that the novel is not only the best, strangest story of the supernatural ever written – head and shoulders

above Mary Shelley's *Frankenstein* or Bram Stoker's *Dracula* – but the first work of art to emerge from horror fiction.[4]

This passage clearly works to lift this popular novel out of circulation: it was discovered 'by chance' rather than because of corporate publicity; it was found not in a multinational-owned mega-bookstore but in a Co-op furniture shop which has now closed down. Ezard relocates this novel in a field of restricted production precisely in order to claim it as 'art' ('the first work of art to emerge from the horror genre') – as opposed to business, or large-scale production – and in turn, to retrieve the concept of an author from the film-of-the-novel, which would seem to have no particular need for that concept. In spite of this, however, Ezard seems to *like* the film, which he claims 'is a remarkably faithful, highly animated version of the original'. The earlier distinction between the private or restricted field of the novel and the public or large-scale field of the film becomes problematic at this point: exactly what *is* being lost when a novel is turned into a film? Ezard's closing paragraph at last comes to the point of the article:

> But there is one wretched difference [between the novel and the film]. The worst of the horror – Lestat toying with a half-drained, terrified prostitute, dancing crudely with the corpse of the plague child's mother – is played as a game for the audience; and the audience at my preview joined in. What I found just about artistically acceptable on the page I watched with a sense of appalled collective degradation in the cinema. It made me long for the years when the tale was little known.[5]

I have already suggested that there never was a time when this particular 'tale' was 'little known': it was always a bestseller. So this paragraph (and much of the article) is more ideological than real in its outline of the 'wretched difference' between novel and film. What it turns on is the suggestion that pleasures derived from a restricted field of production (private pleasures) may be 'artistically acceptable', whereas pleasures derived from a large-scale field of production (public pleasures) are 'degrading' – *even when those pleasures are the same* (since the film is 'remarkably faithful' to the novel). In other words, the same kinds of pleasure produce different effects, depending on whether the form of cultural production is restricted or large-scale. But this view of pleasure simply reproduces the nature of the field of cultural production in its ideological view. Ezard's strangely nostalgic argument seems to be: when pleasure itself is restricted, it can be sanctioned and, more importantly, it can be author-ised, since the author is a concept which is built around a notion of restriction. But when pleasure is *not* restricted (when it reaches a wider audience), it can no longer be sanctioned because a certain loss of author-ity has taken place. The structure of Ezard's relation to the text itself changes radically here: whereas he had identifed the novel through the author, now he identifies the film through the *audience* ('I watched with a sense of appalled collective degradation ... '). The audience here has quite literally done away with the 'author' in the signifying chain: they themselves enable 'the death of the author' to come about. And in fact Ezard's article works very much as a kind of epitaph, mourning the loss of 'Anne Rice' – which also amounts to mourning the loss of one's privacy, a loss attributed here to nothing less than the film-of-the-novel.

But in the actual case of the filming of *Interview with the Vampire*, Anne Rice, as I have said, emerges as an author who simply will not go away. In fact, she had spent over fifteen years negotiating in Hollywood for the film production rights for her novel. One of her particular interests was in who might be cast as Lestat, her 'favourite' vampire: she had suggested Rutger Hauer (whom she had liked in *Bladerunner)*, and later Daniel Day-Lewis, who turned it down. When the film was given to Irish director Neil Jordan, working with producer David Geffen, the role of Lestat was given to Tom Cruise. Anne Rice thought that this was a disastrous choice and she said so somewhat bluntly in an interview with the *Los Angeles Times*: 'Cruise is no more my vampire Lestat than Edward G. Robinson is Rhett Butler.'[6] Now this is not the comment of a novelist who expects to see her novel end up on the shelf of a Co-op furniture shop. The author here 'writes back' to the film, and she does so firstly by moving into the field of large-scale production (the newspaper), and secondly by aligning the film of her own novel with the American popular film epic *Gone with the Wind* – that is, her rejection of Tom Cruise is articulated through a monumentalisation of the film-to-be of her novel, as if this scale of reproduction was its inevitable outcome. (In fact, the film of *Interview with the Vampire* became in its opening week the fourth-highest earning film in the US.) So Anne Rice is an author who does not sit quietly in the field of restricted production. In *People* magazine, Rice went on to say about Cruise: 'I don't want somebody "less clean cut" to play the vampire Lestat. I wanted a great actor of appropriate voice and height who would carry the part – Malkovich, Daniel Day-Lewis, Jeremy Irons. It's a different league. Do any of you actually read? When you're talking Lestat, you're talking Captain Ahab, Custer, Peter the Great.'[7] What I like about these comments is the way they confuse distinctions between popular and high culture – and, for that matter, distinctions between canonised textual heroes such as Ahab and canonised non-textual heroes such as Custer. The complaint 'Do any of you actually read?' may thus have little to do with literature; it precisely responds to her tendency *not* to operate in a restricted field of production.

When the film of *Interview with the Vampire* appeared, Tom Cruise was himself interviewed in a number of populist venues – from *OK! Magazine* (February 1995) to popular film magazines such as *Film Review*, *Premiere* and *Empire*. These venues all work to 'produce' Tom Cruise, to shape him in relation to readers and viewers of the film. In every interview I have read, the article stresses Cruise's 'diplomatic' position on Anne Rice: the actor never stoops to criticise the author. *Empire* called Cruise 'politely diplomatic' when he said of Rice, 'She was opposed to me being Lestat based on other characters that I've played ... She had created Lestat and feels great affinity for this character because of her family, her daughter and what occurred. It was very important to her – but it hurt me.'[8] The author's personal relations to her character are stressed here (the novel was supposed to have been written by Rice in part as a response to the death of her five-year-old daughter from leukemia). But at least the actor is 'hurt' by the author: she has a certain unsettling effect. In the interview in *Film Review*, Cruise noted, 'As an actor I had a great time playing Lestat, but it certainly was unusual to start a movie with someone not wanting you to do it'.[9] So there is a sense here of the actor remaining 'un-authorised' by Anne Rice even as the filming gets underway. This lack of authorisation carries over into Cruise's commentary about the film. In *Premiere* magazine, Rachel Abramowitz asks Cruise about the erotic aspects of his performance as Lestat: '"You're going to have to see for yourself", becomes his standard answer to questions,' she says, 'until he finally gets frustrated: "It doesn't matter what I think about a movie".'[10] What is interesting about this kind of response – a not untypical one for actors – is that it de-authorises the actor's position in relation to the film. The actor is not an author: it 'doesn't matter' what he thinks about his role, although it may matter (to him) what an *author* thinks of his role. What we have with Anne Rice and Tom Cruise in relation to this film, then, is an opposing structure. Whereas Anne Rice intervenes in the filming of her novel by asserting her authorial rights, Tom Cruise withdraws from commentary. In other words, whereas the author uses the film as a means of *refusing* the restricted field of literary production – by occupying more 'available positions' than she might otherwise have occupied as a novelist, by becoming transgressive in this sense – the actor uses the film in order to *maintain* a set of restrictions, sitting 'diplomatically' or conservatively within the frame of an 'available position' defined by his role *as* an actor. The actor is in place as an actor; this means, in short, that he is not an author.

It probably seems like an obvious thing to say: an actor is not an author. But in relation to film, the actor may well carry an 'authorial' role simply by virtue of the fact of his or her visibility on the screen and in screen-oriented media. Actors imprint their own 'signature' on a film, and this signature may be complete enough to erase other kinds of authorial signatures, including the signature of the author of the novel-on-which-the-film-might-have-been-based and, even, the signature of the director (who I shall discuss in a moment). The problem is that the actor's signature in a film is split between the actor himself and the character he plays. Because the actor is engaged (increasingly) in promoting his or her image outside the film itself, he or she is less likely to be taken as the character *in* the film and nothing more. Celia Lury, in her somewhat neglected book *Cultural Rights: Technology, Legality, and Personality* (1993), goes on to note one outcome of this split, where the actor in fact can never be the character precisely because the image marketed outside of film collapses back into the film itself.[11] In a specific sense, the actor can no longer act, meaning that he or she can no longer be anything other than their image outside of the film which casts them in a given role (which may be chosen anyway because of their image). In this way, Tom Cruise can never be anything other than Tom Cruise, as Anne Rice had suggested (although she had also suggested that other actors *could* be the character Lestat). Celia Lury turns to Bruce King's article 'Articulating stardom' (1985) to clarify this point, that acting these days is valued less in terms of impersonation (where the actor disappears into the role) and more in terms of personification (where the role is subordinate to the actor's persona).[12] And yet, when Cruise finally did take up his role as the vampire Lestat, Rice herself enacted an about-face: she claimed that she liked Tom Cruise in the role precisely because, as it unfolded, his acting did in fact privilege impersonation over personification. Notoriously, she took out a two-page, $3,450.00 advertisement in *Variety* (Autumn 1994), in which she stated: 'I was honoured to discover how faithful this film was to the spirit, the content and the ambience of the novel *Interview with the Vampire* ... The charm, the humour and invincible innocence which I cherish in my beloved Lestat are all alive in Tom Cruise's courageous performance.'[13] She is quite specific about what she now values in Tom Cruise: 'I was swept away ... The high point was to see Cruise in the blond hair speaking with the voice of my Lestat. He makes you forget the boyish image of his past films. He is that mysterious and immortal character. I found it an uncompromising movie: I was kind of sick before it came, and I'm cured.'[14] In terms of authorial rights – cultural rights – the point to notice here is not so much the way Rice has revised her earlier claim by suggesting now that Tom Cruise *can* successfully impersonate her character Lestat (to the extent of totally subordinating his own persona), but rather the rhetorical claim she makes *herself* on her character: 'my Lestat'. The actor is subordinated to the character because the novelist says so: it is simply a strategic response to the 'loss' of her character, and the loss of control over her character, at the point of the novel's reproduction as film. Her character Lestat, in other words, is powerful enough to reach beyond the restricted field of the novel – powerful enough to make us 'forget' Tom Cruise.

In fact, Anne Rice was commissioned by producer David Geffen to write the script for the film of *Interview with the Vampire*. She also endorsed Geffen's choice of director, the Irishman Neil Jordan. But Jordan decided to rewrite Anne Rice's script, opening up the distinction between author and scriptwriter (even though the film continued to credit Rice with the screenplay). Jordan claims to have developed the role of Louis, and built up the family relationships between the vampires in the film: 'It's something I had made more central to it than Anne had done.'[15] He also contributed to the screenplay 'a streak of black humour' which, he had said, 'is totally absent from Rice's own work'; and he invested the film with an Irish-Catholic aura.[16] Interestingly, while changing the novel in these and no doubt other ways, Jordan also claimed that he had rewritten Rice's script because 'she wasn't faithful to her own book ... What I had to do was reintroduce aspects of her own novel into the screenplay.'[17] So here, the director is more 'faithful' to the novel than the author: it is one way of authorising his own involvement with the re-directed screenplay. But there was apparently a more banal, institutional reason why Rice continued to be credited with the screenplay, as Jordan 'grumbles' to his interviewer in *Empire*: 'It was put into arbitration with the Writers' Guild and they have rules that if you're a director *and* a writer, you have to prove that you've written 50 per cent of the original stuff to get the credit ... In the case of this, it was impossible because the way in which I changed the screenplay was by taking bits from her novel.'[18] Jordan is more 'faithful' to the original novel than Anne Rice, but he is unable to transgress a clear point of distinction: the director (of a film) is not the author (of a novel). In fact, Adam Mars-Jones, in his review of the film, even de-authorises Jordan's direction: 'Neil Jordan's direction', he says, 'is highly accomplished, without bearing a strong signature.'[19] I would only go on to note that, in quite another sense, Jordan *is* an author: his own novel, *Sunrise with Sea*

Monster, was released at the same time as the film of *Interview with the Vampire*. But there is no overlap between the restricted field of this novel and the large-scale field of the film: they remain distinct, with probably no cross-over audience interest. Rice, however, was publicising her own new novel *Lasher* during the release of *Interview with the Vampire*, and the large-scale publicity she achieved in relation to the film no doubt directly fed into that novel's fortunes.

What I have wanted to suggest in this chapter is that one's relations to the popular are located in the relationship one *already occupies* in, or in relation to, the field of cultural production. One speaks for or against the popular from an 'available position' in that field – a position which enables (or disables) a particular kind of discourse *about* the popular. Obviously, writing an academic chapter with a restricted circulation, I myself am similarly 'positioned' within the field. The academic bears a particular relationship to popular forms of cultural production, usually negotiating a process of enjoyment alongside a process of analysis, the latter in particular depending upon a restricted set of genealogies (one writes an article citing other academics such as Bourdieu, Becker, Lury, etc.) which may have little to do with those popular forms and which may well go unrecognised or unnoticed by them – or if they *are* noticed, those popular forms may, in the sense that Andrew Ross has used this term, have 'no respect' for them. An academic may at best impact upon popular forms just enough to be located in turn by those forms as, precisely, a restricted field of cultural production. I should like to close this chapter by giving as an example a citation from my book *Reading the Vampire* (1994) by the Bristol-based popular film listings magazine *Venue*. This magazine's article on the film of *Interview with the Vampire* has two subsections which are distinguished from the article proper. The first is a selection from Anne Rice's various commentaries on the casting of Tom Cruise and on the film of her novel, entitled 'That Anne Rice volte-face in full'. The second is a column with the more provocative title, 'Cor! So what's it all about then, eh?' This column gives the following advice: 'Impress your chums by memorising these pearls of academic wisdom to regurgitate with suitable intensity after 15 bottles of expensive foreign lager in

your local arts centre bar.'[20] It goes on to quote two short
passages from *Reading the Vampire* about Anne Rice's novel,
and it ends by citing me as the author of that book and an
academic at De Montfort University. It can be an unsettling
experience for an academic to be located in this way – with
what seemed (and still seems) to me to be an instance of
Andrew Ross's 'no respect'. Not to be respected, however, is
not the same as not being noticed: the column ironically
locates or identifies the academic field (the arts centre bar, the
foreign lager, the tendency to want to 'impress' others), but
it also quotes me accurately and at some length, in a bold type
face which is left standing without subsequent comment.
Moreover, I have the feeling that the two passages from my
chapter on Anne Rice were selected not at random, but carefully
and with a certain level of investment in the points being made
– which in fact concern the way Rice builds a 'personal' relationship with a fan audience into the structure of the fiction
itself (a relationship which John Ezard simply reproduces in
his *Guardian* article). In other words, there is both 'no respect'
and *some* respect for the academic in this feature on the film
of *Interview with the Vampire*: the academic is both distinguished or segregated from the interests of the magazine and
included; authorisation is both withdrawn and given. The
mutuality of this arrangement (where the extract is included,
only to be ironised, distanced, etc.) works to produce the
academic response *as* a restricted field of cultural production
(the production of one kind of knowledge about a text). And
yet even this mode of location is not quite watertight. The view
– at least in the popular magazines looked at here – of Anne
Rice's various publicity-seeking statements on the film of her
novel is that she is not 'hysterical' (which might have been
the nineteenth-century diagnosis) so much as *histrionic*. The
word comes from the Latin word for 'actor': the author is an
actor. She gains attention in a theatrical way, in order to
impress others. What I enjoy about *Venue*'s use of my book is
that, tongue-in-cheek, it gives me a similar kind of function:
'Impress your chums by memorising these pearls of academic
wisdom ...'. Histrionics for Rice quite literally contribute to that
author's fortunes by relocating her in a field of large-scale

cultural production, making her transgressive in this sense: she is an author who is out of place because she is making theatrical claims, because she is making the business of acting *her* business. Histrionics, as it is attributed to me, is far less enabling, and it is certainly not tied to (the making of a) fortune. But at least I am given a role to play, minor and comical as it might be, both in *Venue*'s 'arts centre bar' and, more importantly for me at least (since academics value their impact upon the popular, no matter how restricted it might be), in the 'production' of the film of Anne Rice's novel.

Notes

1. Pierre Bourdieu, *The Field of Cultural Production: Essays on Art and Literature*, trans. and ed. Randal Johnson (Oxford: Polity Press, 1993), p. 17.
2. Ibid., p. 17.
3. Fay Weldon, 'Not quite as mad as we are', *Independent on Sunday*, 19 March 1995, p. 27.
4. John Ezard, 'Rice of passage', *Guardian*, 12 January 1995, Screen 14. *Premiere: The Movie Magazine*, February 1995, p. 70.
5. Ibid., Screen 14.
6. Cited in Rachel Abramowitz, 'The vampire chronicles', *Premiere: The Movie Magazine*, February 1995, p. 70.
7. Ibid., p. 71.
8. Jeff Dawson, 'Bloody hell!', *Empire*, February 1995, p. 68.
9. Roald Rynning, 'The vampire interviews', *Film Review*, February 1995, p. 35.
10. Abramowitz, 'Vampire chronicles', p. 71.
11. Celia Lury, *Cultural Rights: Technology, Legality, and Personality* (London: Routledge, 1993), pp. 71–2.
12. Ibid., p. 72; see also Bruce King, 'Articulating stardom', *Screen* 26, 5 (1985), pp. 27–50.
13. Cited in Robin Askew, 'Bestial bloodletting', *Venue*, 20 January–3 February 1995, p. 24.
14. Cited in Abramowitz, 'Vampire chronicles', p. 71.
15. Dawson, 'Bloody hell!', p. 67.
16. Askew, 'Bestial bloodletting', p. 24.
17. Ibid., p. 24.

18. Dawson, 'Bloody hell!', p. 67.
19. Adam Mars-Jones, 'Deathless, ruthless and bloodless', *Independent*, 19 January 1995, p. 25.
20. Askew, 'Bestial bloodletting', p. 23.

3

Is s/he or isn't s/he?: Screening *Orlando*

Nicola Shaughnessy

All the famous novels of the world, with their well-known characters and their famous scenes, only asked, it seemed, to be put on the films. What could be easier and simpler? The cinema fell upon its prey with immense rapacity, and to the moment largely subsists upon the body of its unfortunate victim. But the results are disastrous to both. The alliance is unnatural.[1]

In her 1926 essay on the cinema, Virginia Woolf characterises film as a parasitic, scavenging monster, devouring the body of the text. She presents the novel as a passive, weaker entity. The terms are implicitly gendered: film is the male aggressor, and the literary text its helpless, feminised subject. Despite the imagery, however, this is not nature red in tooth and claw, as Woolf deems film's predatory activity to be unnatural. The cinema's consumption of the novel is presented as a monstrous, vampire-like activity. Woolf then shifts associatively from the relationship between literature and film to that between the spectator and the cinematic text: 'Eye and brain are torn asunder ruthlessly as they try vainly to work in couples.'[2] The conflict that she perceives between visual apprehension and comprehension is central to Sally Potter's 1992 film adaptation of Woolf's novel *Orlando*. It underpins the opening shot of the film, which reveals Tilda Swinton dressed as an Elizabethan courtier, reclining languidly under an oak tree. In voice-over, Swinton quotes the first sentence of the novel: 'there can be no doubt about his sex', but the disjunction between eye and brain, as we see a male character, whilst knowing that it is a woman cross-dressed, establishes from the outset that gender

43

identity is to be viewed sceptically, as a not altogether convincing masquerade. As the omniscient narrative voice continues, 'but when he', Orlando intervenes with a direct address to the camera 'that is, I', thereby reinforcing self-reflexively the sense that his/her gender is a performance.

Given Woolf's strong reservations about the medium, I felt rather treacherous when my first response to Potter's adaptation was an exhilarated celebration of the film text. Several subsequent viewings have done nothing to temper my enthusiasm for it. Contrary to Woolf's concerns, what I perceive in *Orlando* is not an assault upon literature by film but a form of mutual sexual exchange between the primary source and its cinematic other, and between masculinity and femininity in both texts. I would suggest that Sally Potter has brought a maternal perspective to *Orlando*, in an intervention into the fraught relationship between literature and film. Rather than beating the novel into submission and denying its primary source, and in psychoanalytic terms transferring its allegiance from the maternal body (the literary text) to the phallocentric order of film, Potter's version acknowledges and foregrounds its primary source through postmodern, self-reflexive strategies. Thus it gives birth to a new text which is an offspring of its original, but, like Orlando's daughter, looks to its (m)other as she moves into the literary-cinematic future. In this chapter I want to examine three questions: first, the relationship between the literary and the cinematic in *Orlando*; second, the representation of gender in the film text; and, finally, the gendering of the implied spectator.

Running through Potter's *Orlando* is a commentary upon the relations between film and literature. The novel's metafictional musings upon the history of English literature, and upon its own mechanisms of composition, are transposed into a metacinematic framework. At first viewing *Orlando* seems to belong loosely within the genre of costume drama, presenting a synoptic view of English history; on closer inspection, it appears to be more about the mediation of Englishness within literary, cinematic and art history. Woolf's novel is a compendium of literary styles and allusions, and, at one level, Orlando's travels through history trace the trajectory of English literature itself; Potter's version amplifies

and extends this intertextual quality through a density and
breadth of reference which is characteristically postmodern.
The consciously painterly style of the film, the ostentatious
artifice of the visual texture, its elegantly symmetrical and
formalised compositions, its baroque opulence and occasion-
ally surreal detail, provide obvious parallels with the work of
Derek Jarman (especially *Jubilee, The Tempest* and *Carvaggio*)
and Peter Greenaway (from *The Draughtsman's Contract* to
Prospero's Books). The echoes of Greenaway's work are strength-
ened by Potter's conspicuously Michael Nymanesque score, but
the range of cinematic reference is far wider than this. Potter
acknowledges Michael Powell in the end credits, and has
admitted that she 'unconsciously stole from his film *Gone to
Earth*: the scene where she's running in the garden in her
dress'.[3] But there are also hints of Ingmar Bergman in the
moody, icy love scenes with Sasha, of *Lawrence of Arabia* in
the desert sequences, *Brief Encounter* in the parting with
Shelmerdine, and even, perhaps, of *The Great Escape* and *Easy
Rider* in the penultimate scene showing Orlando on a motorbike.
However, the film is also stuffed with literary allusions and
references, far too numerous to catalogue. The opening section
abounds in references to Renaissance poetry, Shakespeare,
and Elizabethan and Jacobean drama. When Queen Elizabeth
first appears it is on a barge which invokes both *Antony and
Cleopatra* and *The Wasteland*, and when Orlando meets her he
quotes Spenser's *Faerie Queene*. Orlando's relationship with the
old Queen (played, of course, by Quentin Crisp), who makes
him a favourite and an object of her desire, invokes the
homoerotics of Marlowe's *Edward II*. The love affair between
Orlando and Sasha proceeds along the lines of an Elizabethan
sonnet sequence, progressing through infatuation with the
unobtainable to jealousy and inevitable betrayal. Having been
abandoned by Sasha, Orlando writes poetry in his mansion
retreat, and is similarly betrayed (in satirical verse) by the
impecunious Robert Greene, who is played by the real-life poet
and dramatist Heathcote Williams (more Jarman intertextuality). The self-referentiality of this performance is also evident
in the casting of the wit and raconteur Ned Sherrin as himself
among the eighteenth-century wits, and in the use of singer
and gay rights activist Jimmy Sommerville to serenade 'fair Eliza'

in the opening moments ('The idea is Jimmy Sommerville parodying Quentin Crisp'[4]): at such moments, the illusion of historical verisimilitude surrenders to a consciousness of its constructed status in the here-and-now.

The interplay between fiction and cinema reaches its culmination in the final sequence, 'Birth', which is linked to the earlier 'Poetry' by the doubling of Heathcote Williams as poet and publisher. Orlando presents her manuscript (the script of *Orlando*, possibly) to a much-spruced up Williams in his docklands office, and he advises her to 'increase the love interest. Give it a happy ending.' This metacinematic touch is part of the overall commentary upon the demise of literature and the ascendancy of cinema. The great house represents the novel, and indeed the heritage of English literature. Even the trees on the drive are covered with dust sheets. The literary echoes throughout the film are like fossils. Literature, for Woolf, is a living entity, but in the film of *Orlando* it is an archaic remnant. Orlando's poetry, and Heathcote Williams's poet, are the subjects of comedy, while the self-conscious posturings of the literary cast of characters, ranging from the three sisters to the Heathcliff/Rochester-like Shelmerdine, present literary history as a picture-book which is quaint but sadly out of date – a branch of the heritage industry. When Orlando's daughter takes the camera in the final sequence, the future of film supersedes the literary past. The film is born out of the novel and transcends it. The last shots of the film, through the viewfinder of a video camera, are shakily managed by Orlando's daughter. Film itself is surpassed by video. The point of view, finally, is that of the next generation.

Amid this promiscuous proliferation of signs, Orlando him/herself can hardly be seen as 'character' in the conventional sense. Both before and after the transformation, Orlando is ill-at-ease in the situation in which s/he is placed, not as a result of personal idiosyncrasy, but as a function of the contradictions within subjectivity that s/he embodies. In the first half of the film this is obviously signalled through the disparity between the genders of the performer and the role, and by Orlando's looks-to-camera (to which I return below), which propel him/her out of the illusionist cinematic space. In such moments, Orlando occupies the position of the voyeur, the commentator or the visitor, rather than that of the participant in history. In the second half, Orlando's alienation is more evidently gendered, readable at the most obvious level, as one reviewer put it, as 'a straightforward parable about a young man who has a rattling good time' which 'turns into a woman who doesn't have such a good time'.[5] In my view, it is not so clear-cut: the female Orlando is for the most part less a 'real' woman than a focus for conflicting ideas of woman, as dictated by the contexts within which 'she' is situated, ranging from the epi-grammatic misogynies of the wits to the claustrophobia of the Victorian era. The figure of Orlando is a series of shifting, conflicting and discontinuous roles, a series of masculine and feminine subject-positions which are successively unable to sustain the burden of signification imposed upon them by the context of the *mise-en-scène*.

In the penultimate sequence, Orlando stands in the midst of tourists in the hall of the great house, looking at a portrait of herself as a young man. This has been preceded by a voice-over which echoes the opening lines of the novel and film: 'she – for there can be no doubt about her sex – is visiting the house she finally lost for the first time in over a hundred years'. This is a reprise of the opening sequence, but in different terms. Orlando is a woman, rather than a man, and a mother. The portrait she studies positions him/her in the historical picture-book frame. The pose is reminiscent of Vita Sackville-West's photographic portraits when she modelled as Orlando for the first edition of the novel. Orlando is thus identified with the past, and with death, which returns us cyclically to the theme and title of the first section.

In this respect, the film is structured around female life rhythms, and thus can be read in terms of Kristeva's notion of 'women's time', whereby 'female subjectivity would seem to provide a specific measure that essentially retains repetition and eternity from among the multiple modalities of time known through the history of civilisations.[6] The episodic structure of the film reinforces this, in spite of the chronological order derived from the novel. This is not 'time as project, teleology, linear and prospective unfolding; time as departure, progression and arrival', which Kristeva identifies with masculine structures.[7] There are two modalities of time operating in *Orlando*: historical time and cyclical time, with the former subordinate to the latter. During the episode entitled 'Politics', the monarch changes – almost imperceptibly. Orlando presents himself to the Khan as 'a representative of His Majesty's government'. When the Archduke Harry arrives, several minutes and several short scenes later, he announces himself as an 'emissary from Her Majesty'. The gender of the monarch has switched, just as the gender of Orlando switches towards the end of this section. 'Repetition' and 'eternity', through which Kristeva characterises female temporality, are thematic and structural features of both film and novel. However, the novel *Orlando*, as a (mock) biography of Vita Sackville-West, betrays an anxiety which is central to the novel's form and subject. As Clare Hanson points out:

> To textualise a person is to fix them, to appropriate them, in a manner which might well trouble Woolf. Yet beneath this level of concern over appropriation, there is a deeper sense of unease evidenced in the text which might relate to Kristeva's notion of 'abjection'. To write a person into a text is to translate them into a medium which is neither living nor dead and thus perhaps to transgress or unsettle the fixed boundary between life and death and evoke the experience of abjection.[8]

Vita's name means life, and in writing *Orlando*, Woolf was perhaps endeavouring to make her subject eternal through her textual life. I find it interesting that, in the novel, birth and death seem to be avoided, but in the film version these are the terms which frame the entire narrative. In the final sequence, critically, Orlando could be dying, and this was certainly my interpretation when I first saw the film. According to Potter, the intended effect was more ambiguous:

> It seemed to me that *Orlando* was, at its heart, a celebration of impermanence. Through the vehicle of Orlando's apparent immortality, we experience the mutability of all things and relationships ... the film ends on a similar metaphysical note to the book, with Orlando caught somewhere between

heaven and earth, in a place of ecstatic communion with the present.[9]

This temporal and spatial ambiguity is, however, part of the underlying concern with gender identity. The figure of the angel hovering in the sky is poised literally between heaven and earth. The angel is Jimmy Sommerville, the falsetto who sang earlier in the film for Queen Elizabeth as she travelled up the river, supposedly four hundred years previously.

This gender-bending, as a male actor sings with a feminine voice, is, of course, central to the shifting subjectivities of the film. Potter explains:

> the longer I lived with Orlando and tried to write a character who was both male and female, the more ludicrous maleness and femaleness became, and the more the notion of the essential human being – that a man and woman both are – predominated.[10]

Ludicrous is an interesting term, as this is precisely the word I would use to describe my discomfort with the image of the angel in gold who disrupts the final scene in an obviously postmodern metacinematic device which foregrounds the artifice of the film's methods. The gaudy amateur theatricality of this device is like a ludicrous last-night joke, lifted from Potter's live performance work. (It also refers to the 'stormy weather' sequence of Jarman's *The Tempest*.) Is it a comment on the impossibility of filming Woolf's text? It certainly prevents a sense of closure at the end of the film; narrative, like the angel, is left suspended. Faced with Orlando's unblinking stare at the end of the film, I felt no sense of the ecstatic dissolution of difference that Potter proposes. Nor is it an androgynous site of sexual communion, despite Sommerville's shrill assurances that 'I am coming'. Potter writes that 'at the moment of change, Orlando turns and says to the audience "Same person ... different sex." It is as simple as that.'[11] It is certainly not as simple as that.

'Is s/he or isn't s/he?' is a central question throughout the film, in a complex interplay between cross-dressed male and female actors. Early in the film, Tilda Swinton and Quentin

Crisp are involved in a dressing-room scene of intense theatricality and queasy voyeurism. Orlando watches the Queen
undressing; his eyes are averted, looking away from the Queen
and, initially, from the gaze of the camera, indicating his
discomfort with the spectacle. Orlando's unease with his role
as voyeur is shared by the spectator. Playing upon our consciousness of the male body beneath the Queen's clothes, the
editing of this scene plays games with what can and cannot
be seen whilst sustaining the cross-dressing convention. As she
starts to disrobe, the camera shifts us discreetly outside the
bedchamber: we watch Orlando looking (and not looking) at
the off-screen spectacle. When Orlando returns our gaze, it is
a mute appeal, as if he has seen, or is about to see, something
forbidden, even monstrous (the body of the mother?). In the
bedchamber scene that follows, the gender relations between
the aged Queen and the youthful courtier are dynamically
altered by the transvestitism: Crisp as Elizabeth simultaneously
embodies both patriarchal and matriarchal power, while
Orlando's fictive masculinity is repositioned in terms of
sexualised subjection to the Queen. Remembering that the title
of this section is 'Death', the contrast between Elizabeth's
ghastly pallor and Orlando's clear skin and flushed cheeks is
especially striking in this scene: we are presented with a dis-
concertingly ambiguous picture of sexual (and political) power,
exploitation and subordination.

   The direct address to the camera, used in this scene, is a device
which is deployed repeatedly to transgress gender norms. The
jealousy of Orlando's fiancee Euphrosyne when she witnesses
his/her attentions to Sasha causes her to throw her ring at
Orlando and proclaim 'the treachery of men'. Orlando, as the
published script has it, '*turns to camera with a slightly guilty
expression, which changes to one of light bravado*',[12] and in a direct
address declares 'it would never have worked. A man must
follow his heart'. We are made conscious of Orlando's
performance of masculinity. The look to camera is traditionally a male preserve: from Oliver Hardy to Michael Caine (in
Alfie), it is a gesture of complicity towards a spectator who is
presumed to be male. Here, the duplicity of the aside draws
attention to the woman playing a man. We are conscious of
the *double entendre* in Orlando's statement, but the irony desta-

bilises the precarious sense of gender identity that Tilda Swinton as Orlando inhabits.

The irony is compounded by the fact that Swinton returns the gaze of the spectator whenever there are doubts about gender identity. During his courtship of Sasha, Orlando witnesses a performance of *Othello* on a makeshift stage on the frozen Thames. At the close of this performance, the actor playing Othello kisses the boy actor playing Desdemona and, falling on the bed, dramatically 'dies'. Orlando pauses, then turns to the camera to whisper 'Terrific play'. A terrific play on sexual identity it is. In the subsequent scene, we observe Orlando's despair when he is abandoned by Sasha. Again, he looks at the camera to declare 'the treachery of women'. The Sasha episode plays on desire and eroticism in the sexual encounter between two female performers. The spectator is presented with close-ups of Orlando caressing Sasha. The directions in the script are explicit: '*Orlando lifts his head and moves his mouth across her cheek to her mouth. They kiss slowly and sensually.*'[13] The ostensibly heterosexual encounter clearly has a lesbian subtext. However, this duality does not quite match the hermaphroditic fantasy of Woolf's text. Woolf presents Sasha in the following terms:

> The person, whatever the name or sex, was about middle height, very slenderly fashioned, and dressed entirely in oyster-coloured velvet ... But these details were obscured by the extraordinary seductiveness which issued from the whole person ... Legs, hands, carriage, were a boy's, but no boy ever had a mouth like that; no boy had those breasts; no boy had eyes which looked as if they had been fished from the bottom of the sea.[14]

In Potter's script, she is introduced as '*a dark slender figure dressed in furs*'.[15] But there is nothing particularly boyish about Charlotte Valandrey's Sasha, who during her first conversation with Orlando is rendered in soft focus and becomingly lit by candles; if anything, her femininity is emphasised in order to make explicit the interplay between female heterosexuality and lesbian eroticism.

I find Orlando most convincing as a man in a wig. In the 'Politics' section, where he is in ambassadorial costume, Orlando becomes a comic figure whose clumsy posturings ridicule the behavioural codes of nation, class and gender. Orlando betrays his/her vulnerability as, staggering, he drinks to 'manly virtues' and 'brotherly love'. In this section masculinity is explicitly connected with arrogance and violence. Orlando's compassion for the dying man, and regret when he hears the crying babies, trigger his transformation into a woman. For Potter, this transformation 'is a result of his having reached a crisis point – a crisis of masculine identity'.[16]

Orlando is equally uncomfortable in the female costume she is forced into after her metamorphosis. In a reprise of the scene of Queen Elizabeth's undressing we see Orlando being straitlaced into corsets, confining her body and fixing her into a conventional feminine identity. Her escape into marriage is transformed by Potter into a love affair with an American, 'the voice of the new world – the romantic and revolutionary view of the beginning of the American dream'.[17] Potter cast Billy Zane as Shelmerdine because he combined the looks and presence of a matinee idol ('He's very Errol Flynn') with 'slightly androgynous beauty'.[18] Even in the most heterosexual part of the film, sexual identity is still in flux. This is reflected in the camerawork. During their conversation, there is a shift from the conventional male–female, shot-reverse-shot formula to fluid panning between the two speakers. As desire and gender ambiguities become the subject of the dialogue, the position of the spectator itself oscillates (a similar effect is seen in Orlando and the Khan's toasting scene, which is infused by an implicit homoeroticism). The scene then shifts to Orlando and Shelmerdine in bed, and the camera surveys a body, the identity of which is uncertain, moving slowly over the flesh until it rests upon an eye which returns the gaze of the spectator. Although this is Orlando's eye, it is interesting to note that when I first watched the film I thought it was Shelmerdine who was looking at me at this point. The male friend I was with, however, identified the eye as Orlando's immediately.

This brings me, finally, to the question of how the reader is gendered by this film text. What is the identity of the implied spectator and whose 'pleasure' does it cater to/for? To address these questions I want to return finally to the pivotal moment of both literary and cinematic texts – the transformation of Orlando. This is effected through a sleeping beauty scene, where Orlando wakes up after seven days sleep, takes off his wig, and reveals her long woman's hair. After two short, sensual shots of Orlando washing, she surveys herself in a long, keyhole-shaped mirror (echoes of Botticelli's *Birth of Venus*). We share her own full-frontal view of her body. Thus, whereas in the novel, Orlando's metamorphosis is achieved through a grammatically and logically 'impossible' sentence – 'He was a woman' – it is in the film effected through the disclosure in a mirror of the female body. 'Same person. No difference at all', says Orlando, and then turns to the camera with a change of voice: 'Just a different sex.'

How are we to read this moment? At one level, the exposure of Orlando via the spectacle of the female body seems to endorse Laura Mulvey's well-known theorisation of the dominant cinematic apparatus in terms of 'woman as image, man as bearer of the look'.[19] At such a moment, female subjectivity is coterminous with the sexualised body. As the *Sight and Sound* reviewer, Lizzie Francke, noted: 'Orlando is never seen naked in his male incarnation – he is never authenticated as a man, rather he remains effeminately boyish.'[20] Practical considerations aside, the point is, of course, that within the terms of conventional filmic representation, Orlando is not authenticated in this manner because he does not have to be: the female Orlando *is* her body in a way that the male Orlando is presumed not. And yet the effect of this pivotal moment is more ambiguously subversive than this, not least because we are positioned with Orlando as she confronts her own mirror-image. Importantly, the shot of the naked Orlando is actually very brief, and it is both preceded and followed by sustained close-ups of Orlando looking at her mirror-image. Quite clearly and emphatically, it is the female subject who has ownership of the gaze at this crucial moment: a point which is underlined by her triumphant look to camera that ends the sequence. It is this calm, confident act of looking that re-appropriates the image from the domain of male sexual fantasy and offers the possibility of an empowering, pleasurable and non-masochistic identification for the female spectator.

Notes

1. Virginia Woolf, 'The cinema' (1926), *Collected Essays*, vol. 2 (London: The Hogarth Press, 1966), p. 269.
2. Ibid., p. 269.
3. Sally Potter quoted in David Ehrenstein, 'Out of the wilderness: an interview with Sally Potter', *Film Quarterly* 47, 1 (1993), p. 4.
4. Ibid., p. 6.
5. Jonathan Romney, 'Baroque and role-reversal', *New Statesman and Society*, 12 March 1993.
6. Julia Kristeva, 'Women's time', in *The Kristeva Reader*, ed. Toril Moi (Oxford: Basil Blackwell, 1986), p. 191.
7. Ibid., p. 192.
8. Clare Hanson, *Virginia Woolf* (Basingstoke: Macmillan, 1994), p. 96.
9. Sally Potter, *Orlando* (London: Faber and Faber, 1994), p. xiv.
10. Ibid., p. xiv.
11. Ibid., p. xv.
12. Ibid., p. 16.
13. Ibid., p. 17.
14. Virginia Woolf, *Orlando: A Biography* (1928; London: Granada, 1977), pp. 23–4.
15. Potter, *Orlando*, p. 12.
16. Ibid., p. xi. B. Ruby Rich makes a similar point in a discussion which interestingly contrasts *Orlando* with the recent cinematic preoccupation with violent masculinity (as evidenced in *Reservoir Dogs*): 'Orlando's mythic transformation from man to woman occurs at the exact moment in which he is required to enter into battle and kill' ('Art house killers', *Sight and Sound*, December 1992).
17. Potter, *Orlando*, p. xii.
18. Potter, quoted in Ehrenstein, 'Out of the wilderness', p. 5.

19. Laura Mulvey, 'Visual pleasure and narrative cinema', *Screen* 16, 3 (1975), reprinted in Gerald Mast, Marshall Cohen and Leo Braudy (eds), *Film Theory and Criticism: Introductory Readings*, 4th edn (Oxford: Oxford University Press, 1992), pp. 750ff.
20. Lizzie Francke, 'Orlando', *Sight and Sound*, March 1993.

4
Feminist Sympathies Versus Masculine Backlash: Kenneth Branagh's *Mary Shelley's Frankenstein*

Heidi Kaye

In *Mary Shelley's Frankenstein*, Kenneth Branagh attempts to create a *Frankenstein* for the 1990s. On one thematic level, the film offers a feminist interpretation of the text by stressing the issues surrounding motherhood and women's roles, which follows two decades of such readings of the novel. Yet on another level, Branagh's version recreates the gendered polarities which feminist readings of the novel argue are undermined by Shelley. Instead of critiquing the way Victor's act of creation symbolically kills off the female, Branagh's film can be seen to recapitulate Victor's 'crime' by emphasising male/male relationships over male/female ones, reinforcing women's role as token of exchange in essentially homosocial relationships.[1] This chapter will consider both the inter- and extra-filmic aspects of these competing themes.

First of all, I'd like to consider some of the main changes Branagh's *Frankenstein* makes to Mary Shelley's story in order to investigate the significance of his different emphases. Most noticeably, he expands the role of Elizabeth and makes explicit the importance of motherhood. The other important changes lie in the main male characters surrounding Victor: his father, Waldman, and the Creature. While the changes involving the female characters serve to stress the feminist elements in the story, those involving the male characters bring out the theme of father/son relationships. Branagh develops the feminist reading of *Frankenstein* by reading into the story Mary Shelley's own life. As various feminist critics have done (notably

57

Ellen Moers, Mary Poovey, Sandra Gilbert and Susan Gubar, Margaret Homans, and Anne Mellor),[2] although rather less subtly, Branagh produces a semi-biographical interpretation informed by feminist readings of the text. The death of Shelley's own mother, Mary Wollstonecraft, in childbirth becomes in the film Victor's mother's death giving birth to his brother William; this in turn gives rise to Victor's desire to create life from death. In the novel, Victor's mother dies of scarlet fever after nursing Elizabeth through the disease. Shelley's own experience of losing her first child within two weeks of its birth (compounded later by the death of another of her children) and her horrific dream of its revival ('Dream that my little baby came to life again; that it had only been cold and that we rubbed it before the fire, and it lived. Awake and find no baby. I think about the little thing all day. Not in good spirits.'[3]) have been read into the novel's concerns for non-reproductive creation and/or reanimation of the dead. Branagh's film shows him using amniotic fluid and a semi-sexual mechanism (to which I shall return) to bring life to the dead Creature.

In addition, Mary Wollstonecraft's Enlightenment feminism is brought into the film through the expanded role of Elizabeth. In the novel, she plays a very minor part, acting only as a love interest and, even worse, is viewed by Victor as a possession. She is presented as a 'pretty present' from his mother as a child:

> I, with childish seriousness, interpreted her words literally and looked upon Elizabeth as mine – mine to protect, love, and cherish. All praises bestowed on her I received as made to a possession of my own ... my more than sister, since till death she was to be mine only.[4]

Elizabeth as played by Helena Bonham-Carter is represented as an equal to Victor, intelligent, passionate, with a sense of humour and a strong will. This was a key decision for Branagh, as he states:

> It was important to me to have a very strong woman's role in a film of this size ... and I wanted Elizabeth and Victor to be two equal partners, utterly entwined from the beginning. These two people were absolutely meant to be together.[5]

Bonham-Carter's Elizabeth is Mary Shelley and Mary Wollstonecraft rolled into one: rational, emotional, independent,
expressive. She seeks out Victor in Ingolstadt to convince him
to come home; when he refuses because he must complete his
work, she boldly offers to help him. Nowhere is her strong will
and independent mind more clearly portrayed than in the final
sequences of the film. On their wedding night, Elizabeth is
equally as lustful as Victor, rather than 'the purest creature of
earth' (III, 6, 189), and when Victor reanimates her using parts
of Justine's body, Elizabeth refuses to be a party to her objec-
tification and sets herself on fire with the kerosene lamp.

I'd like to look at this scene in a bit more detail. Victor, after
removing the reborn Elizabeth from the sarcophagus, dresses
her in her wedding dress, complete with ring on the hand that
was Justine's, and sits her down on a crate like a limp rag doll.
He kneels before her, imploring her to remember him: 'Say my
name. Please, you must remember. Elizabeth ... Elizabeth.' The
screenplay stage directions state: *'She lifts her head to look at
him. A flicker in her eyes? His saying "Elizabeth" seems to have
triggered some memory.'*[6] He helps her to stand, encouraging her
to remember, and then begins what the screenplay calls *'the
most sweepingly romantic and hair-raisingly demented image of the
film'* (*MSF*, p. 131) when Victor dances with the Creaturess
Elizabeth, while the camera swirls crazily around them and the
waltz theme madly plays in Victor's head. At the peak of the
action, it crashes to a halt as the Creature appears in a flash
of lightning.

A showdown between the two men over the woman is
inevitable. The Creature says 'She's beautiful' and Victor replies
'She's not for you'. The Creature beckons to Elizabeth, who is
drawn to him, while Victor calls out 'Elizabeth? ... say my name
...'. The Creature calls 'Elizabeth' and tells her 'You're beautiful',
whereas Victor keeps desperately asking her to 'Say my name'
(*MSF*, p. 132). It is not surprising that it is to the Creature that
she goes in this scene. It is he who has been calling her name
and telling her she's beautiful, whereas Victor has been self-
centredly asking her to remember him, not herself. If she
remembers who she is, or who she is supposed to be, she may
well reject what he has fashioned her into. When the scene
turns into a literal tug of war, where the viewer may well

expect that the two men will tear an arm or hand off the patchwork woman, Elizabeth finally comes to a recognition of the situation, cries out and breaks free of them both. After a mime of attributing blame to Victor for recreating her as a monster, she snatches up the lamp and crushes it between her hands, throwing flaming kerosene all over herself. She wants no part in these men's games with life and death, and she refuses to be possessed by either of them; she creates her own destiny.

The film emphasises, as the novel does, the gendered split between the public and private realms, the university and the home. Branagh's film uses strong contrasts of colour to portray the Frankenstein home as harmonious and happy, with bright blues and pinks, wide open spaces such as the ballroom and the Alps, and plenty of natural light. The domestic world is safe and comfortable, innocent and cheerful. In direct opposition is Ingolstadt, portrayed in shades of umber and grey, with miserable, starving peasants and enclosed spaces such as the circular lecture theatre and Waldman's secret laboratory. The only vast space, Victor's attic workshop, is dark and crowded with looming equipment, like some nightmare factory. The domestic sphere is the realm of the family, gendered female by Elizabeth's dominating presence as receiver of Victor's ever-scarcer letters home. The university is dominated by men, students and professors, and is the site from which Victor rejects his home and family for his scientific work. Although we lose the parallel with Waldman's situation as explorer of the unknown outside world, since he does not write letters to his sister in England (as in Shelley's text), he does make clear the opposition at the end when asked by his first mate which direction they should go and he replies 'Home' (*MSF*, p. 139). Elizabeth stands out as she runs through the streets of Ingolstadt in her red clothes; she does not belong in this world barren of colour and domestic affection. The red obviously symbolises blood: menstrual, from birth, and also from death; she will be carried home a corpse in a flowing red shawl. Red and blood are therefore female, and life and death are connected in this way with femininity; but this is a power that Victor wants to claim for himself, without the intervention of women.

The other major emphasis in Branagh's film is on the father/son relationships. In contrast to the feminist reading of Elizabeth and the will to recreate motherhood, through the father/son dynamic Branagh recreates a world of male/male relationships that are primary and which exclude or threaten the female, just as Victor does in Mary Shelley's story. There are three relationships on which I want to focus here: Victor and his father, Victor and Professor Waldman, and Victor and the Creature. Unlike in the novel, where he is a bourgeois gentleman, Victor's father in the film is a doctor. This establishes a goal for Victor to follow in his father's footsteps, even to exceed his father's success: 'You'll become an even greater doctor than your father', says his mother (*MSF*, p. 42). His father kills his mother during childbirth; Victor resurrects his own wife. Or another way to look at it is that his father's child kills his wife; Victor's 'child' kills his own. Both women are, in either case, tokens to be saved or killed to represent something about their men. Victor's mother is self-sacrificing – 'Cut me. Save the baby' (*MSF*, p. 43) – and Elizabeth kills herself – her biggest self-assertion is in self-annihilation.

Even more important is the relationship Victor has with Professor Waldman. Other Frankenstein films have also increased the role of scientific mentor figures, most notably James Whale's *Frankenstein* (1931) in which the mad scientist is called Dr Pretorius, who returns in *Bride of Frankenstein* (1935) to blackmail Henry Frankenstein into creating another Creature. In both of these films, Frankenstein is presented as less guilty because of the power of the older scientist who leads him into the unhallowed experiments. Whereas in the novel, Victor is obsessed and alone in his studies, with even Henry Clerval left back in Geneva since his merchant father will not allow him to attend the university, in the films Victor almost always seems to need an assistant, which helps lessen his sole responsibility for the Creature and its deeds. Shelley's character isolates himself from his family and friends, and even from the university authorities, to conduct his research, and comes up with the answer by himself. Branagh's character learns from Waldman some of the arcane knowledge, eventually stealing his secret research journal to discover how far he got in creating life and adapt his methods. He tries to involve Clerval in his research, but he refuses, raising the moral grounds that are brought out by the hindsight narrative in the novel: 'Even if it were possible, and even if you had the right, which you don't, to make this decision for us – can you imagine for one second that there wouldn't be a terrible price to pay?' *(MSF*, p. 69).

Waldman, with his flowing grey hair and intense, sinister mien, makes for a dangerously seductive mentor. From the moment they lay eyes on each other, the two men seem mutually fascinated. As his coach drives away after Victor's first lecture and confrontation with Professor Krempe over the purposes of medical study, Waldman stares out of the window at Victor; Victor returns his look, full of curiosity: 'Who was that?' *(MSF*, p. 59). When Waldman invites Victor and Henry into his private laboratory, the professor is impressed at Victor's ability to rescue Henry from the out-of-control monkey's arm. Victor offers to help Waldman in his research; the two men exchange intense looks, and Waldman seals their private bond with 'You shall, of course, tell no one' *(MSF*, p. 65).[7] Victor is distraught when his mentor is killed, so preserves his great mind by transplanting his brain into the body of his murderer. This not only adds to the link between Victor and Waldman and intensifies that between Creature and Creator, but also spreads the responsibility for the Creature's actions to Waldman. Unlike in *Young Frankenstein* (1974) and some other versions, the Creature's brain cannot be excused as 'abnormal'; instead, it is a highly superior model, intelligent and humane, with a sense of moral responsibility since Waldman had abandoned his experiments in reanimation. The Creature is both victim and killer, intellectual and peasant, related to both Victor and Waldman as spiritual and physical fathers.

An even more tangled father/son dichotomy occurs between the Creature and his Creator in this film, partly because of the age difference between De Niro and Branagh; the Creature states after Victor's death, 'He was my father' *(MSF*, p. 137). Certainly, Victor stands in the father's position in this relationship, which is underlined by the creation sequence in which the two men scrabble about amidst the amniotic fluid, with Victor trying to help his Creature to stand. Yet even in this scene, the size of the Creature and the slipperiness of the floor are such that it appears that both are having equal difficulty in gaining their feet and each is essentially helping to support or drag down the other as they alternately rise and fall again.

This potential for a reversal of roles is made manifest in the ice cave scene. Here, when Victor is confronted by an eloquent (despite the Bronx accent) and sensitive Creature, we see what might appear to be a father/son discussion, but this time the Creature seems to have taken the father's role. The Creature has dragged Victor out of the pool and when he awakes he finds a fire lit and the Creature inviting him over for a chat. The Creature presents his case rationally and effectively dresses down young Victor for his irresponsible behaviour:

> You gave me these emotions, but you didn't tell me how to use them. Now two people are dead. Because of us. Did you ever consider the consequences of your actions? (*beat*) You gave me life, and then left me to die. (*beat*) Who am I? (*MSF*, 115–16)

In this scene, the only shot of the two characters in the same frame is the establishing one, showing them at opposite ends of the cave. Once Victor comes up to the fire, the shot switches to alternate close-ups of one character then the other. This emphasises the distance in their relationship at this stage, with Victor rejecting his child and the two in conflict after the Creature has killed William. The older actor adds authority to the role of the Creature, making him able to lecture Victor in this way and convince him to create a mate for him. The young Victor asks his Creature simply, 'What can I do?', and accepts, despite his immediate horror, his responsibility: 'If it is possible to right this wrong … (*beat*) … then I will do it' (*MSF*, pp. 116–17).

Outside the film, the choice of De Niro to play the Creature creates a similar father/son dynamic. Once again, there are multiple father/son combinations in the film's production. The chapter on 'The filmmakers and their creations' in *MSF* notes this father/son, American/British relationship, without irony: 'TriStar Pictures soon added its considerable weight as the *parent* studio' (*MSF*, p. 145, my italics). Francis Ford Coppola, fresh from his own *Bram Stoker's Dracula* (1993), produced the film, adding Hollywood clout and money and his own theatrical style to the picture. A director/producer father figure for Branagh, Coppola is an older film-making mentor as well as an attractive bet for American audiences, backed by a major Hollywood studio. Although in his interview with *Empire*, Branagh claims that it was he who sought De Niro to play the Creature, *MSF* states that it was the producer (Coppola, along with a string of production executives) who were 'pursuing' De Niro in order 'to land' him for the part, as well as seeking Branagh as director since Coppola chose not to direct this project (*MSF*, p. 145). Thus the creative hierarchy is rather more complex: is Branagh seeking a father/mentor or is Coppola seeking a son/heir to hand this project on to him? Coppola claims to have 'discovered a kindred spirit in Branagh: "... I recognized in him some of the same kind of energy and competence to do whatever it takes that I fancied I had myself, also coming out of the theater"' (Coppola, quoted in *MSF*, p. 147). Branagh takes up his role equally: 'For his part, Branagh was appreciative of the older film-maker's "supportive presence" on the set and behind the scenes, saying, "I'm grateful for the opportunity to have a genius looking over my shoulder"' (*MSF*, p. 147).

De Niro is an acting mentor of the same generation as Coppola, from a different tradition than Branagh's, who offers a certain amount of artistic seriousness and American pulling power to his film. Branagh says of him in his publicity material that he needed 'an actor of great courage and brilliance'; De Niro returns the compliment by saying of Branagh in his fatherly role of director, 'Ken understands how actors like to work and how they talk'.[8] Branagh admits to being excited and somewhat starstruck by both men before and after making the picture: 'It was a trip. (*Long pause.*) It was a *trip*. Coppola, I just wanted to soak up all his stories ... So to meet De Niro in the same day was too much, frankly.'[9] These American filmic father-figures help legitimise Branagh's project and enable it to be produced on such a large scale and high budget. Yet the film is presented as 'A Kenneth Branagh film' or as 'Kenneth Branagh's *Mary Shelley's Frankenstein*', just as we had 'Francis Ford Coppola's *Bram Stoker's Dracula*'; it is assigned as the creation of patriarch Branagh even over its original female author.[10]

These father/son relationships both inside and outside the film compete directly with the motherhood and strong woman themes. It is not surprising that the locket which William carries and which leads to his death at the Creature's hands is now a portrait of Victor, rather than one of his mother, as it is in the novel. Victor as father/brother has replaced the importance of the mother. The enormous sack containing the electric eels that get injected into the sarcophagus of amniotic fluid at the moment of recreation looks like a gigantic scrotum. The screenplay itself describes it as 'a huge bollock-shaped container' (*MSF*, p. 78). The sexual imagery is therefore explicitly male: the sperm-like eels are ejaculated down the glass tube from the bollock-shaped container into the waiting sarcophagus to bring to life the Creature. The human-sized fish kettle is called a sarcophagus and is certainly not womb-shaped, rather it is likened to a coffin, which indicates the death-dealing aspect of this motherless method. Victor's deadly asexual reproduction method has short-circuited the system, eliminating the need for the female principle; hence the film prioritises male/male relationships even over the main male/female one between Victor and Elizabeth. Derek Malcolm in the *Guardian* accurately writes, 'The film seems to think Frankenstein's love for Elizabeth carries the same weight [as the Creature's relationship with Victor]. It doesn't.'[11] The two men, Victor and Creature, compete for power as alternate father and son, just as they fight over the body of Elizabeth/Justine. The women are, despite the attempt to retain independence, merely ciphers, who can act as replacement parts for each other.

Victor's journal is a posthumous present from his mother, expected 'to be filled with the deeds of a noble life' (*MSF*, p. 50). It is filled with Victor's experimental notes and inherited by his 'son', the Creature, who finds it in the pocket of Victor's greatcoat. From it, the Creature learns of his 'accursed origins' (II, 7, 126) and discovers where to find his lost 'father', in Geneva. The mother is once again written out of the story, since the Creator/Creature link is much stronger than the mother/son one, despite the fact that it is supposedly his mother's death that spurs Victor's research in the first place.

Mary Shelley's book is similarly 'written out' of the film's story, despite its title. Although some of the film's publicity claims that the title *Mary Shelley's Frankenstein* was chosen to indicate the film's intention to return to a more 'faithful' adaptation of the novel, in reality the title was a necessity, since Universal still own the copyright of the title *Frankenstein* used in the 1931 James Whale version. The same was true for *Bram Stoker's Dracula*. Branagh's film brought along with it the expected literary tie-ins, including a Macmillan edition with De Niro and Bonham-Carter on the cover. In addition, the takeover of Mary Shelley's novel continued with a 'novelisation' of the film, written by Leonore Fleischer and called *Mary Shelley's Frankenstein*. Finally, there is the text to which I have been referring throughout, *Mary Shelley's Frankenstein: The Classic Tale of Terror Reborn on Film*, with Branagh credited as author of the book, which includes the screenplay by Steph Lady and Frank Darabont, a director's note, a biographical note on Mary Shelley, Branagh's introduction to the screenplay, information on the film-makers, an afterword on the Creature, and a rather brief *Frankenstein* filmography (describing a mere 17 of the more than 110 film versions of the story). Kenneth Branagh's name appears above, albeit in smaller letters than Mary Shelley's, but that is mainly because the title of book and film are *Mary Shelley's Frankenstein*, so it is the book's title that is larger than Branagh's name, not Shelley's name standing as itself. Information on the philosophy of the production abound, overshadowing the film script itself; thus once again Branagh as director takes precedence over Shelley's tale. Nevertheless, as some of the above discussion has shown, Branagh does seem to reassert more of the original themes of the novel, as well as introducing elements from its author's biography. The publicity material and most of the newspaper coverage stress Shelley's life and the circumstances of the novel's creation, including the story of her dream of the monstrous creation which she tells in her 1831 preface. In emphasising this, Branagh is again seeking authority in his film; it is to be much closer to the 'real' story and 'real life', not just another horror film, but a 'serious' adaptation of a literary work for the

1990s. Shelley herself told the tale of the events leading to her creation of the story in the preface to the revised edition of 1831 in order, as Christopher Frayling claims,

> to turn them into a cliffhanger, to reinterpret her own novel which had proved controversial in religiously orthodox terms, and to provide a suitably melodramatic curtain-raiser to a story which had already acquired a reputation as a piece of theatrical blood and thunder. The preface was, most likely, a canny piece of marketing.[12]

Marilyn Butler, in her preface to the recent edition of the 1818 text for Pickering and Chatto, argues that Shelley's preface as well as her changes to the novel were designed 'to fend off possible charges of materialism or blasphemy' by making it 'a substantially different and less contentious novel'.[13] This mixture of titillation and conservatism in Shelley's revision can be seen in the combination of feminist and masculinist concerns in Branagh's version.

Branagh himself is described in several articles on the film as an obsessive and driven director, not unlike his character, Victor Frankenstein. Helen Hawkins and George Perry in the *Sunday Times* criticised his 'semi-hysterical direction', and Geoff Brown in the *Independent* described him as 'equally wild-eyed as director and Victor Frankenstein'.[14] Certainly the director offers a kind of god-like power over the actors, as Branagh said appreciatively of De Niro: '"He would do what I asked and put himself into my hands"' (*MSF*, p. 151). Several critics could not resist the chance to remark along the lines of 'Branagh has created a monster'.[15] Some comment was caused by the creation sequence, in which Branagh appears stripped to the waist, his newly acquired pectorals oiled and gleaming (his personal trainer gets a credit, as does De Niro's). David Thomas in the *Sunday Times* half-seriously asks whether Branagh, despite his superior acting talent, was trying to compete with the likes of Mel Gibson and Keanu Reeves in the body department: 'Did we really need to see those newfound muscles, that hard-earned torso, that suggestive patch of stomach hair?' He sees it as a sign of the universal attention-seeking ego of actors.[16] This is a rather more significant issue, since Branagh's muscle-bound scene reinforces the male bonding/competition themes in the film, rather than the romance theme. Competing with the action heroes in physical attributes, Branagh's semi-nakedness is not represented as heterosexual. He is showing off for the boys, not the girls. Since this scene ends up in a semi-nude struggle with the Creature, it recalls the naked wrestling match in Ken Russell's *Women In Love* (1969), with all of its homosexual connotations. Julie Burchill writes, 'Branagh claims he intentionally made [it] homoerotic'.[17] Whether or not this is true, Victor's naked chest is on display in this scene, and simply emphasises his muscular masculinity at the moment of his creative act. Both the text and Victor are masculinised by this expectation of male bonding and male viewing.

Shelley's novel has been seen as a book born of other books, responding to Milton, her parents', Percy Shelley's, and other works crucial to the Romantics and her own literary interests. Childbirth and writing are both creative processes linked by Mary Shelley in the novel. Branagh continues in the same vein as he appropriates the novel for his own creative purposes. The description of his turning the novel into a film echoes Victor's desire to probe the hidden secrets of nature in his search for the secret of life: 'As Branagh thought his way into the story, *discovering more and more of its unexplored dimensions*, it became clear to him that certain themes needed to come out in the screenplay' (*MSF*, p. 146, my italics). Are these dimensions unexplored by Victor, by Shelley, by previous film-makers? What enables Branagh to discover them, when others have not? He, like Victor, seeks to uncover what is hidden and thereby display his genius, even more than Shelley's. The crucial addition of a scene where Victor reanimates Elizabeth builds up her role only to force her into self-immolation. Ironically, in his male egotism/hero-worship as director and actor and in his emphasis on homosocial relations over heterosexual or mother/child relations, Branagh seems to recreate, at least to some extent, the 'abomination' abhorred by Shelley through the character of Victor, recapitulating the (virtual) elimination of the female from representation in the patriarchal order.

Notes

1. In this way, the film can be read via Eve Kosofsky Sedgwick's theories about homosocial bonding and male-male-female triangles. See *Between Men: English Literature and Male Homosocial Desire* (New York: Columbia University Press, 1985).
2. It is a vast oversimplification of the work of these critics to say that they encourage a semi-autobiographical reading. However, in that they do interpret the text as representing female experience, especially that of Mary Shelley, such a broad generalisation will serve for this comparison. See Ellen Moers, *Literary Women* (New York: Doubleday, 1977); Kate Ellis, 'Monsters in the garden: Mary Shelley and the bourgeois family', *The Endurance of Frankenstein*, ed. George Levine and U.C. Knoepflmacher (Berkeley: University of California Press, 1979), pp. 123–42; Mary Poovey, *The Proper Lady and the Woman Writer: Ideology as Style in the Works of Mary Wollstonecraft, Mary Shelley, and Jane Austen* (Chicago: University of Chicago Press, 1984); Sandra Gilbert and Susan Gubar, *The Madwoman in the Attic: The Woman Writer and the Nineteenth-Century Literary Imagination* (New Haven: Yale University Press, 1979); Margaret Homans, *Bearing the Word: Language and Female Experience in Nineteenth-Century Women's Writing* (Chicago: University of Chicago Press, 1986); Anne Mellor, *Mary Shelley: Her Life, Her Fiction, Her Monsters* (London: Methuen, 1988).
3. Mary Shelley's journal, 19 March 1815, quoted in Moers, *Literary Women*, p. 147.
4. Mary Shelley, *Frankenstein* (Harmondsworth: Penguin, 1985), based on the 1831 edition, I, 1, p. 35. All further references will be included in the text.
5. Kenneth Branagh, quoted in 'Mary Shelley's Frankenstein: Production Information', 1994, p. 6.
6. Kenneth Branagh, *Mary Shelley's Frankenstein: The Classic Tale of Terror Reborn on Film*, with the screenplay by Steph Lady and Frank Darabont (London: Pan, 1994), p. 130. All further references will be included in the text as *MSF*. Darabont is described in the text as 'a great fan of the

Shelley novel', which supposedly gives him the right credentials 'to make a film that was truer to Mary Shelley, both in letter and spirit, than any preceding version, but that spoke directly to today's audiences', *MSF*, p. 145. Although often considered as a canonical 'literary' text, *Frankenstein* has 'fans', which might make it seem more like a popular novel. See Ken Gelder's discussion, in this volume, of the idea of the fan in relation to the author.

7. See also Julie Burchill, 'Charge of the fright brigade,' *Sunday Times*, 6 November 1994, section 10, p. 6, who sees this as a 'sexy' relationship.

8. Kenneth Branagh and Robert De Niro, quoted in 'Mary Shelley's Frankenstein: Production Information', 1994, pp. 5–6.

9. Barry McIlheney, 'Mission accomplished?', *Empire*, December 1994, p. 103.

10. Lizzie Francke also notes this search for 'respectability' and 'legitimacy', 'Creatures great and tall', *Guardian*, 27 October 1994, G/2, pp. 8–9. Barry McIlheney goes to the extreme of this parental authorisation nomenclature by referring to the film as '*Francis Ford Coppola's Kenneth Branagh's Mary Shelley's Frankenstein*, to give it its full, wonderful title', p. 100.

11. Derek Malcolm, 'Stitched up and let loose', *Guardian*, 3 November 1994, G/2, p. 12.

12. Christopher Frayling, 'Monstrous regiment', *Sunday Times*, 10 April 1994, section 7, p. 1.

13. Marilyn Butler, 'The first *Frankenstein* and radical science', *Times Literary Supplement*, 9 April 1993, p. 12.

14. Helen Hawkins and George Perry, 'Film check', *Sunday Times*, 27 November 1994, section 10, p. 54; Geoff Brown, 'Coffin and spluttering', *Independent*, 3 November 1994, p. 37.

15. *Variety* is amongst these: 'Branagh has indeed created a monster, but not the kind he originally intended'; Hugo Davenport writes, 'Brankenstein's monster may thus be a hybrid in more than the intended sense, bringing bits of himself from the far side of the Atlantic', 'Branagh Hatches a Patchy Monster', *Telegraph*, 4 November 1994; slightly more original, the *Evening Standard* writes,

'Branagh's new film adds up to considerably less than the parts' (quoted in Giles Whittell and Dalya Alberge, 'Film Critics Savage Branagh as Prince Woos Tinseltown', *The Times*, 3 November 1994, p. 3).

16. David Thomas, 'Spare us the parts', *Sunday Times*, 4 December 1994, section 9, p. 21.
17. Burchill, 'Charge of the fright brigade', section 10, p. 6. In contrast, Suzi Feay sees this scene as simply 'a moment of parent-child bonding', 'Mother to the Monster: With Kenneth Branagh's New Film, Frankenstein Walks Again', *Independent on Sunday*, 6 November 1994, Books.

5

The *Henry V* Flashback: Kenneth Branagh's Shakespeare

Deborah Cartmell

Kenneth Branagh, dubbed in *The Times* on the day before *Henry V*'s release in 1989 as 'the young pretender', claimed that the play needed 'to be reclaimed from jingoism and World War Two associations'.[1] Without doubt, Branagh's film pays homage to Laurence Olivier's film of 1945 while seemingly rewriting the history for a 1980s audience. As Graham Holderness has argued, Olivier's *Henry V*, sponsored by the Ministry of Information, was designed as a morale-boosting exercise, in keeping with the dominant Shakespeare criticism of the period. Holderness has illustrated how in the 1940s Wilson Knight's *Olive and the Sword* and E.M.W. Tillyard's *Shakespeare's History Plays* view Shakespeare as a spokesman of national unity.[2] In the words of Wilson Knight, writing in 1943, 'we need expect no Messiah, but we might, at this hour, turn to Shakespeare, a national prophet if ever there was one, concerned deeply with the royal soul of England'.[3] In this chapter, I will examine how Branagh's film blends popular culture with academic nostalgia and succeeds in reaching, to use Branagh's own words, 'a large group of potential Shakespeare lovers'.[4]

In his production of *Henry V*, Kenneth Branagh reverses many of the editorial decisions of Olivier; most notably, not to appear anti-Europe, he turns the French into worthy opponents and even makes the Dauphin a likeable figure. As with all film versions of Shakespeare, speeches have to be reduced in order to make the plays filmic – the long speeches freeze the action and can be boring to watch. As in the Olivier version, Branagh's Chorus is fragmented so that a few lines punctuate the action rather than suspend it. On the rare occasions when speech does suspend action, it has a shock effect on the audience. Such is the case of Judi Dench's rendering of Mistress Quickly's account of Falstaff's death and Michael Williams's delivery of his namesake Michael Williams's rebuke to the king, suggesting that Henry's cause is unjust and his word untrustworthy. Here we have close-ups, concentrating on the suffering of the individual and hanging a question mark over the ethical position of the King. Henry himself achieves this intense visual scrutiny in his desperate prayer to the god of battles on the eve of Agincourt. Initially it would seem that the close-ups are used by Branagh to question rather than approve the King's actions. Certainly, unlike Olivier's production, Branagh's film is striking for its *inclusions* rather than its exclusions.[5]

Perhaps the most notable of these inclusions are the sentencing of the conspirators and the hanging of Bardolph (which Branagh shows rather than simply has reported). Branagh also includes flashbacks to the *Henry IV* plays, depicting Falstaff and crew in the tavern, ostensibly to suggest Henry's betrayal of his comrades. The flashbacks are used again with the hanging of Bardolph and in the final moments of the film. Flashbacks function in Branagh's film by abruptly offering new connotations to the narrative, the process which Roland Barthes calls the 'semic code'.[6] Initially these flashbacks seem to function to discredit or call into question Henry's imperialist ideology.

The film begins with Henry presented as ruthless, distrustful and potentially evil. He tricks the conspirators and the atmosphere is one of tension – there are spies everywhere and the King can only maintain his position through subterfuge. The archbishops, unlike the ineffectual jokey figures of Olivier, are conspiring together, hardly holy figures, but shrewd and corrupt politicians. The King enters the film literally cloaked in darkness, forecasting the disguised King on the eve of the Battle of Agincourt. For a 1980s audience, the inhuman black masked figure inevitably recalls Darth Vader in *Star Wars* (1977), and thus the audience is invited to regard the King – as does Michael Williams in the later scene – with the utmost suspicion. Like the Olivier film, Branagh takes the image of doors opening to visually connect different scenes. (The dark figure of Henry (seen from behind) framed by a door is used in the publicity posters for the film.) Branagh underlines the fact that this is a Henry capable of opening doors, in the Machiavellian sense of using his position of power to seize every opportunity. As if by magic, the doors open for the King at the beginning of the film (preparing us for the opening of the gates of Harfleur), and they close on Scroop and his fellow conspirators in Southampton. While Renee Asherson in Olivier's film is confined within doors and like a damsel in distress is liberated from the effete French by the heroic Olivier, Emma Thompson's Catherine opens the door to discover a gloomy and desperate world of her care-worn father (played by Paul Schofield whose French King visually recalls his portrayal in Peter Brook's *Lear*).

This dark side of Henry is in direct contrast to Olivier's Christian warrior king and is undoubtedly the product of the influential revisionist readings of the mid 1980s, most notably Stephen Greenblatt's 'Invisible bullets' and Jonathan Dollimore and Alan Sinfield's 'History and ideology: the instance of *Henry V'*. The picture of Branagh's Henry at the beginning of the film is in keeping with Stephen Greenblatt's account of a Henry who 'deftly registers every nuance of royal hypocrisy, ruthlessness and bad faith – testing, in effect, the proposition that successful rule depends not upon sacredness but upon demonic violence'.[7] Branagh seems to do to Olivier what Dollimore and Sinfield do to E.M.W. Tillyard in attacking the notion of a natural hierarchical order in Shakespeare. Dollimore and Sinfield consider *Henry V's* strategies of power and its representations in which the human cost of imperial ambition is revealed through Henry's own ideological justifications.[8] This is most apparent in the play text in Henry's exchange with Michael Williams when Henry tries to rid himself of the responsibility of war; although the disguised Henry insists that the King will keep his word, he later fails to keep his word to Williams – the glove is returned without the promised fight, subtly confirming Williams's assertion that Henry, because he *is* a king, will not be true to his word. Henry, in this respect resembles Machiavelli's ideal prince; and this episode is very close to Machiavelli's chapter on why a prince should (not) keep his word.[9] Fluellen's historicising of Henry's war (the continual comparison of his prince to ancient predecessors suggests Machiavelli's own method of analysis) results in an unintentional truth: Fluellen notes that Alexander 'did in his ales and his angers, look you, kill his best friend' (IV, vii, 34–5).[10] Although the comparison stops here for Gower – 'Our king is not like him in that. He never killed any of his friends' (IV, viii, 36–7) – in denying the likeness he affirms it. Inevitably the comparison recalls Henry's sentencing of Scroop ('that knew'st the very bottom of [Henry's] soul') and of course Falstaff (who the 'king hath run bad humours on').[11]

The chiaroscuro effects of the dark beginning of Branagh's *Henry V* hark back to Orson Welles's *Chimes At Midnight* (1967) in which Welles's Falstaff is incrementally reduced and brutalised by a self-aware and self-serving Prince Hal. Branagh's throned Henry visually recalls John Gielgud's cold and isolated Henry IV, the Darth Vader (or dark father) of Welles's film. Through a series of intertextual references – flashbacks to other plays and films – the film initially seems to build a picture of Henry who is hostile and repellent. The close-up and flashback, however, rather than questioning his motives, ultimately soften and humanise the figure. When Bardolph is being hanged, Branagh has Henry recall through flashback the ribald days of the tavern while the close-up reveals his eyes to be moist – the tears blending with the rain. After the prayer to the god of battles in which Henry acknowledges his father's guilt in taking Richard's crown, there are definite tears in the King's eyes, and in his union with Fluellen after victory he's clearly weeping. The vulnerability of the King in this scene is contrasted with and compared to the slaughtered boys. As David Robinson notes on the eve of the film's UK release: 'Branagh's Henry is strictly according to the Geneva Convention'.[12] The image of the King carrying the dead boy – a former companion of his 'wild Hal' days and a victim of his dubious war[13] – provides the emblem of the film, used in many of the publicity pictures: it visualises the ambivalence of this production which simultaneously glorifies and condemns Henry's war. Youth has been sacrificed; the King emerges at the end of the film as a 'real man'.

The film doesn't inspire feelings of nationalism, as in the Olivier film, but rather, as Graham Holderness remarks, Branagh's film conveys the *emotions of patriotism*.[14] But these emotions grip you unaware. The first third of the film is markedly anti-war and anti-patriotic; but by the end, the audience should be cheering the King alongside his rebel ranks (like the opportunistic and corrupt Pistol and Nym who can't help but feel inspired by the St Crispen Day speech).

It is often noted that the film, made in the late 1980s and following the lead of Adrian Noble's 1984 production (in which Branagh played the title role), is a post-Falklands, anti-war production. The realism of the piece is in direct contrast to the painted scenery of Olivier's version (with the exception of the fanciful scene depicting the English coast behind the Chorus: Derek Jacobi looks as if he's literally standing on a map of Great Britain).[15] Branagh imitates and pays tribute to Olivier, following in his footsteps by commencing his film career, like Olivier's, by directing and starring in *Henry V*, a play which appropriately dramatises a young man's rite of passage. The St Crispen's day speech offers a clear visual flashback to Olivier – Branagh uses a cart, like Olivier, as a humble platform for his rousing words. Likewise, Branagh imitates or rivals Olivier in the hail of arrows fired in unison by the British footsoldiers at the beginning of the battle sequence.

The film, however, also pays tribute to contemporary Vietnam war films which present a simultaneous fascination and contempt for war.[16] Chris Fitter has argued that through the rhetoric of class transcendence, Branagh's film conveys the double message that war is hell but it also heroises.[17] Unlike Olivier's *Henry V*, Branagh's film was not paid for by the government but was made in spite of reduced subsidies. Branagh's own company, Renaissance Films plc, shows how success can be achieved, like Henry's war, against all the odds. It gained a BAFTA and Academy Award and made money (approximately seven and a half million pounds). Quick on the heels of the film's critical success, Japan's giant Sony Corporation made an investment in Renaissance Films.[18] Branagh's Henry V, unlike the aristocratic characterisation of Olivier, reveals throughout his working-class Belfast origins; he is the epitome of the self-made man who rises from the common ranks through sheer entrepreneurialism. In his auto-biography, *Beginning*, Branagh underlines the similarities between himself and Shakespeare's king when he first undertook the role at Stratford: 'Henry was a young man, and so was I. He was faced with an enormous responsibility. I didn't have to run the country and invade France, but I did have to control Brian Blessed and open the Stratford season.'[19] During the filming of *Henry V*, Branagh was inevitably prone to making comparisons between his and Henry's predicament. In fact, his diary of the shooting reads like a rewriting of Shakespeare's play, climaxing in Branagh cutting his Harfleur wall-shaped birthday cake. Henry-like, he continually underlines the risks he was taking in embarking upon the project: 'As the nights wore on there were less people available, and the shooting schedule had to be planned so that we covered as much large-scale action as possible early in the week, before it really was a case of we few, we very, very few.'[20] On returning home after the filming of the battle sequence, Branagh writes 'I felt as if I had come back from the war'.[21] Branagh's identification is with a king who has more in common with Richard Branson than Winston Churchill – he seems to have grown out of an age of football hooliganism and the conquest of privatisa-tion. Eventually Henry is transformed into the ideal 1980s man: rugged, yet a lover of children, confident yet self-mocking. Clearly, this Henry struck a chord: contemporary reviews are full of praise for the inspirational tone of the production. Allegedly Prince Charles – Patron of Branagh's company – cried.

The Chorus – a seemingly inappropriate figure for a film – is retained by Branagh, as he was by Olivier, to manipulate our reactions and engage us with the action. In the play text, Shakespeare's Chorus calls attention to the inadequacies of theatre, continually reminding us that we are watching a play. Branagh's Chorus, played by Derek Jacobi, dressed in a modern replica of a First World War trench coat, introduces the play on the film set as if he were the director. Initially he seems cynical and detached. As the action develops, his emotional involvement builds – in fact, a careful viewing of his face at the end of the film reveals a scar, as if he has directly partici-pated in the Battle of Agincourt.[22] He literally changes face and this conversion from cynical observer to enthusiastic recruit mirrors the *volte face* of the film as a whole.

Harold Innocent's Burgundy suggests a bald-headed, con-servative politician, a cross between Churchill and the then soon to be British Arts Minister, David Mellor. Visually and verbally he ties all the loose ends together; the flashbacks accompanying his lament for the wastes of war while concentrating on the victims of Henry's reign, provide the audience with a filmic curtain call, inviting us to savour the glorious moments of the film. In Olivier's film, Burgundy, played by Valentine Dyall, mournfully looks out of a painted window and the fairy-tale landscape, based on Pol de Limbourg's illustrations, is exchanged for a contemporary picture of two children, reflecting Burgundy's images of ruin and devastation: 'Even so our houses and ourselves and children / Have lost, or do not learn for want of time, / The sciences that should become our country, / But grow like savages'.[23] Surprisingly, we find ourselves in 1945 rather than 1420. Unlike Valentine Dyall's Burgundy, Harold Innocent's Burgundy is ultimately determined to look on the bright side; there is a sense of satisfaction in what has been achieved rather than lost in war. Rather than looking *forward*, this Burgundy looks *backward* – not to the ravages of war (as in the Olivier version) but back to images of merry England. The audience is invited first to mourn and then applaud the jolly faces paraded before them. Similarly, Branagh's film looks backward – while appearing to oppose Olivier's patriotic glorification of war and nationalisation of Shakespeare, it ultimately applauds it, reaffirming the myth of 'authentic Shakespeare'.

Initially, Branagh's film seems to call attention to the play's ironies, seemingly interrogating Henry's dubious political premises. But, if anything, Branagh's film is more a product of right-wing ideology than is Olivier's. While Olivier daringly pierces the illusion of stability in Burgundy's elegiac speech bringing the film audience into their own time, Branagh takes us back in time, cunningly consolidating Shakespeare as an ideological force, reaffirming the views of critics like E.M.W. Tillyard, Wilson Knight, and those responsible for teaching within the National Curriculum. The fighting spirit of the British combined with the eternal words of the Bard provide an ideal British export, a force to be reckoned with (or marketed) abroad.

The British National Curriculum Council consultation reports continue to put Shakespeare top of the list of reading for tests for 14-year-olds. The unimaginative and tedious nature of the exam questions was the focus of a series of conferences in 1993[24] aimed to combat the testing of Shakespeare as spokesman of Tory ideology (Nigel Lawson, for instance, claimed that Shakespeare is a Conservative through and through). In vehemently opposing the Shakespeare tests, a leading poet and dramatist was moved to say that Shakespeare is the only religion left to us. She objected to the government institutionalising and claiming authority over the Shakespeare Faith. She was backed by the majority of teachers present who agreed that Shakespeare should, in effect, be privatised: he must not be confined to a single correct reading, endorsed by the government, but Shakespeare – like God – is for everyone. Even the less able (or the less impressed) should be allowed contact with him. The teacher's role is an evangelical one, and in this respect not far removed from the preachers of English in the 1920s and 1930s who believed that everyone could 'gentle their condition' through exposure to the uplifting language of great literature, epitomised by the works of Shakespeare.[25]

To return to Branagh's film, it could be said that it is designed with an eye to providing a marketable teaching resource, a teaching resource which inspires appreciation (rather than 'understanding') of Shakespeare. Branagh's mission is to convert us firstly to Henry and then to Shakespeare. The religious atmosphere of the end of the film, reinforced by the City of Birmingham Symphony Orchestra's *Non nobis*, is a point which is hard to miss. The music, which begins with the mournful tones of a single singer and ends with a rousing chorus and orchestra (similar in effect to *Land of Hope and Glory*) combines the forces of spiritual celebration and national anthem, paying tribute to Shakespeare's (and Branagh's) achievement. Wilson Knight's words are worth requoting here as they are, surprisingly, more akin to the ultimate message of Kenneth Branagh in 1989 than of Laurence Olivier in 1945: 'we need expect no Messiah, but we might, at this hour, turn to Shakespeare ...'.[26]

Notes

1. *The Times*, 5 October 1989.

2. Graham Holderness, *Shakespeare Recycled: The Making of Historical Drama* (Brighton: Harvester Press, 1992).
3. *The Olive and the Sword*, (Oxford: Oxford University Press, 1944) p. 3.
4. Branagh, *Beginning* (1989; reprinted New York: Norton), p. 236.
5. It is, nonetheless, worth noting that when comparing Branagh's *Henry V* to Olivier's, our first impression is to note the inclusions, but compared to the play text, as Robert Lane outlines in '"When blood is their argument": class, character, and historymaking in Shakespeare's and Branagh's *Henry V*', *English Literary History*, 61 (1994), pp. 27–52, Branagh, like Olivier before him, evades a number of chinks in Henry's ideological armour, among them:

    i.   Pistol's comments that the 'world is "Pitch and pay". / Trust note, faiths are water-cakes' (II, iii, 44–5) is left out.
    ii. Fluellen's historical analogy of Alexander and Henry in that they both killed their best friend (IV, vii, 20–37) is missing from Branagh's text.
    iii. Much of Henry's disclaimer of his responsibility for war to Williams is cut (IV, i).
    iv. Pistol's ransom scene with the French soldier is eliminated (IV, iv).
    v.   Branagh removes the boy's complaint that Pistol lives while Bardolf and Nym are dead (IV, iv).
    vi. The scene in which Henry refers to Williams's challenge and offers him payment is cut (IV, viii).

6. See Maureen Turim, *Flashbacks in Film: Memory & History* (New York and London: Routledge, 1989).
7. 'Invisible bullets', *Shakespearean Negotiations* (Berkeley and Los Angeles: University of California Press, 1988), p. 56.
8. Jonathan Dollimore and Alan Sinfield, 'History and ideology: the instance of *Henry V*', in John Drakakis (ed.), *Alternative Shakespeares* (London: Methuen, 1985), pp. 206–27.

9. The message is 'but since men are a contemptible lot, and would not keep their promises to you, you too need not keep yours to them', trans. Machiavelli, *The Prince*, Mark Musa (New York: St Martin's Press, 1964) Chapter XVII, p. 145.

10. All references to *Henry V* are taken from the Oxford edition, ed. Gary Taylor (Oxford: Oxford University Press, 1995).

11. II, ii, 94; II, i, 116.

12. *The Times*, 5 October 1989.

13. Critics have often referred to the dead boy as 'anonymous', yet it is Christian Bale, the actor who plays the boy of the tavern company. The mistake is easily made as it is, strangely, hard to identify Bale in the long tracking shot of Branagh carrying the dead boy across the battlefield (see K. Branagh, *Beginning*, p. 236).

14. Holderness, *Shakespeare Recycled*, pp. 191–2.

15. There are, nonetheless, a few unintentional seams in the film's realism, such as Branagh's 1980s hairstyle (which in no way resembles the famous crop of Henry V); Branagh's hair seems to have been washed and blow dried in between cuts of the Harfleur sequence. At one point it is muddied and flattened, while a few moments later it has been restored to its earlier glory.

16. See Holderness, *Shakespeare Recycled*, p. 200.

17. 'A tale of two Branaghs: *Henry V*, ideology, and the Mekong Agincourt' in Ivo Kamps (ed.), *Shakespeare Left and Right* (London: Routledge, 1991), p. 270.

18. Lisa Buckingham, *Guardian*, 30 January 1990, p. 9.

19. Branagh, *Beginning*, p. 141.

20. Ibid., p. 228.

21. Ibid., p. 236. Reviews of the film, similarly, make such an identification. For example, Stanley Kauffmann, in 'Claiming the throne' (*New Republic*, 4 December 1989), writes: 'Possibly he sees an analogy between that army [i.e. Henry's] and Britain today and possibly thinks that, through this film, he – a young man – can help quicken morale in a country that is self-confessedly dispirited' (p. 30).

22. This is also noted by Peter Donaldson, 'Taking on Shakespeare: Kenneth Branagh's *Henry V'*, *Shakespeare Quarterly*, 42, 1 (1991) pp. 60–70, at p. 63.

23. V, ii, 56–9.

24. Theatres', Universities' and Schools' Conference on Shakespeare, Birmingham, London and Durham, March 1993.

25. See, for example, George Sampson, *English for the English*, first published 1925.

26 Knight, *Olive and the Sword*, p. 3.

6

Consuming *Middlemarch*: the Construction and Consumption of Nostalgia in Stamford

Jenny Rice and Carol Saunders

When the BBC decided to film *Middlemarch* at Stamford in the summer of 1993 they were creating opportunities for the re-packaging of culture as nostalgia which could be consumed in a variety of ways. Stamford, as a location, rather than the 'real' setting of Coventry,[1] reflected a sanitised, nostalgic perception of nineteenth-century town life, focusing on grand Georgian villas, wide crescents and narrow lanes with quaint bow-fronted shops. Recontextualising a nineteenth-century novel as a television programme transforms traditional relationships between production and consumption. In its place we find an intertextuality of elements all available to be consumed. From conventional souvenirs to 'expert seminars', from behind-the-scenes videos to weekend breaks run by national hotel chains, there is an eclectic range of consumer activities. Our analysis will consider how this Stamford-as-Middlemarch experience is symptomatic of postmodern culture. The quest for nostalgia is Janus-faced: at once backward-looking, a search for self-identity in a more certain past, and forward-looking, providing an opportunity for the emergent service class to access the dominant culture.

George Eliot's *Middlemarch*, subtitled *A Study of Provincial Life*, was shown on BBC TV during the first two months of 1994. It marked the BBC's return to costume drama, a genre neglected for nearly five years. Andrew Davies transformed nearly eight hundred pages into six episodes, each of which had an audience averaging five million.[2] These ratings ensured the genre's revival, with *Persuasion* and *Pride and Prejudice* continuing the trend.

85

The choice of Stamford rather than Coventry enabled the production team to represent *Middlemarch* in a 'real' setting that resonates with our nostalgic images of Georgian Britain. It was selected for two reasons: first, the number of intact streets with 1830 and pre-1830 buildings; and second, these areas could be blocked off and insulated from outside traffic noise.[3] The BBC had expected to select many locations all over the country. As producer Louis Marks indicates, they assumed they would film:

> a street here, a square there, a house somewhere else. But then our researchers came back and told us they had found this marvellous town that had everything ... and ... they were right. Stamford is beautiful. Extraordinary.[4]

Stamford is now as identified with Middlemarch as Castle Howard is with *Brideshead Revisited* and Holmfirth is with *The Last of the Summer Wine*. This association mobilises consumer demand for nostalgia as spectacle, a feature of postmodern culture.

Nostalgia has been defined as a 'sentimental yearning *for* (some period of) the past'.[5] As Robert Hewison reminds us, 'nostalgic memory should not be confused with total recall', for unpleasant events are filtered out.[6] Many writers (notably Wood, Hewison, Strong) have sought to explain the preoccupation with nostalgia as a retreat from an uncertain present.[7] In part this uncertainty can be linked to the structural and cultural changes of postmodernism which can explain the current preoccupation with nostalgia and its consumption. Three key transformations have influenced the development of postmodern nostalgia: a dissolution of common cultural heritage, de-differentiation, and consumerism.

The age of postmodernity, while freeing individuals from past ideological constraints, has resulted in uncertainty about social and cultural identity, characterised by 'a loss of the social roots and the dissolution of a common cultural heritage that has normally shaped identity and self-concept'.[8] The nostalgic representation of Middlemarch created in Stamford can become that lost cultural heritage. Therefore to 'consume'

Middlemarch in Stamford as a commodity is one way of actively promoting self-identity.

Postmodernism not only involves a dissolving of boundaries between cultural forms such as tourism, television, shopping and architecture; but also within cultural spheres there is a merger described by Urry as de-differentiation. This involves the merging of high and low culture and the 'breakdown of some ... of the differences between the cultural object and the audience'.[9]

Televising classic novels for mass-audience consumption is an example of this merging of high and low culture. Writing in the *Guardian* (12 April 1995), Fay Weldon claimed that while sales of the book *Middlemarch* rocketed when it was televised in 1994, this did not imply an increase in George Eliot readers: 'most people, it is now said, opened the first page, read, and put it promptly down'.[10] Whilst there may be a reluctance to engage with the 'high culture' of the written text, the TV series is seen as having mass appeal. In the past (and for some today) reading was seen as a more worthy activity. Weldon nails her colours to the postmodern mast when she says:

> But times have moved on and now I see the matter differently. I no longer regard reading as necessarily superior to viewing. 'Viewing' has developed its own resource, its own history.[11]

Urry's recognition of the narrowing of the distance between cultural object and audience can be seen in the consumer orientation to Stamford-Middlemarch. This, together with the merging of high and low culture, raises the issue of the constituencies of such consumers. The process of consuming Stamford-Middlemarch is an example of the third key post-modernist transformation – consumerism, understood in this chapter, as a response to the transformations of cultural heritage and de-differentiation. It addresses the first issue of self-identity by filling the gaps left by the dissolution of cultural identity. As Rob Shields suggests there is a need:

> to treat consumption as an active, committed production of self and of society which rather than assimilating

individuals to styles, appropriates codes and fashions, which are made one's own.[12]

Furthermore, an implication of the de-differentiation between cultural object and audience is that there is more audience participation.[13] This is shown at Stamford in the range of experiences which are available for consumption. Illustrated talks, weekend breaks, Blue Badge guided tours and town trails continue to engage tourists. With sales worldwide to 24 countries, more international visitors are experiencing Stamford-Middlemarch.[14]

We suggest that these three key postmodern transformations are all implicated in both the production and consumption of the nostalgic Stamford-Middlemarch experience. In the process of filming the TV drama, Stamford was reconstructed as Middlemarch through a range of production and consumption relationships, some persisting long after the filming and first public showing took place.

Stamford became the location for the creation of a lost cultural heritage. This was initially achieved through the set designs of the production designer, Gerry Scott, who recreated an 1830s Middlemarch from 1993 Stamford. Whilst recognising the importance of historical accuracy, Scott's aim to convey the essence of the period rather than to focus on small details underlines an attempt to create a nostalgic rather than a faithful reconstruction. With the emphasis on creating an identifiable cultural heritage, there was, nevertheless, a selection process that, in this case, privileged the characters over the visual authenticity and this necessarily produces a tension of legitimation. Thus in her desire to foreground the characters, she preferred to decorate buildings and interiors with colours from the less obtrusive Georgian palette rather than the stronger Regency tones.[15]

Cultural heritage was further promoted when after the production of the drama a variety of consumable souvenirs were marketed as cultural heritage artefacts. These include typical examples such as postcards of the filming in the town (over 30,000 have been sold), notebooks, coasters and bookmarks and two videos of the making of the TV drama: an official BBC video for media studies students and an unofficial video of a bystander's view.[16] These are perhaps examples of the direct 'spin-offs' from the drama produced for the tourist industry. However, the production of consumables has also been exploited by traders less immediately connected to the heritage business. Middlemarch biscuits have been made by a local man tailoring his production to suit tour events. It is even possible to taste a 'Middlemarch Curry' ('offer extended for Middlemarch visitors'), an international dimension which has been popular with local residents rather than tourists.[17]

The crucial difference between the 'official' souvenirs and the commodities such as the biscuits and curries is that the latter reveal the more postmodern distinction of blurring of boundaries. Official souvenirs signify their status through identifiable signs; commodities such as the curry do not operate within this signifying system. Yet the two forms of commodities can be said to function within the same cultural sphere: a characteristic of de-differentiation, referred to earlier. It is not only commodities that show this key transformation. Other examples include the privileging of discourses, such as character to visual authenticity; and the unofficial video which captures the process of filming in a 'real' location: a jumble of 1830s streets with characters in period costume, and 1990s cars, women pushing baby buggies and actors smoking, perfectly demonstrates the blurring of distinctions between production and consumption and between cultural object and audience. These examples could be described as 'jumbling', identified by David Harvey as one of the 'more pervasive characteristics' of postmodernism.[18] The significance here is the way that such images contribute to shaping the past for contemporary viewers: a past in which Middlemarch and Stamford have themselves become 'jumbled'. The production of the TV drama and artefacts may contribute to creating a nostalgic common cultural heritage that could offer consumers a focus for developing a shared sense of identity.

The filming of *Middlemarch* was not responsible for bringing tourism to Stamford, already a hub of cultural interests with its arts centre, tourist office, museum, local stately homes and an annual Shakespeare festival. However, *Middlemarch* shifted the focus to a more participatory activity. As the owner of a dress shop indicates, 'The only difference is the people come to see Middlemarch rather than Stamford'.[19] Moreover, tourists' visits have become more experiential; in post-Fordist terms this is an example of the commodification of experience. Commodities are used up as they are consumed or involve the purchase of time and, as such, are potentially renewable.[20] At Stamford they are offered activities to participate in which blur the distinction between the two towns and encourage tourists to experience Stamford as Middlemarch. The museum town trail, entitled 'Stamford as Middlemarch', traces a route between all the main sites of buildings used for filming. A 'replica' map of Middlemarch superimposed on the actual town plan of Stamford is also available. This is drawn in nostalgic terms with Georgian buildings throughout the town (there is no sign of the new shopping centre) and decorated with horse-drawn coaches and Coats of Arms. The name 'Middlemarch' dominates the map in calligraphic lettering while the name 'Stamford' is drawn in less impressive lettering at the bottom. This map is being sold in aid of the Macmillan nurses' appeal, an example of how charities are widening their promotional activities.

Many other souvenirs and experiences articulate the link between the towns. Parallels are drawn in the booklets on sale at the *Stamford Mercury* offices. A pamphlet entitled, 'Middlemarch Revisited – Election Fever', includes a facsimile of the *Lincoln, Rutland and Stamford Mercury* for 13 August 1830, charting Election Reform fever. Even an educational activity such as the Museum Curator John Smith's lecture, 'Stamford and Middlemarch: two towns in 1830', focuses on politics and medicine, themes relevant to both Stamford and *Middlemarch*. Smith describes a realistic account of 1830s society in contrast to the many commercial ventures which give a sanitised vision of life in an early nineteenth-century town.[21]

The growth in tourists in search of Middlemarch is contributing to the production of Stamford as a heritage spectacle where the divisions between the 'real' and the 'fake' become confused. The visitors are not only audience but in some sense actors too; as they follow the town trail or guided tours they can experience going around 'Middlemarch', itself a fake. In some cases the visitors even seem confused as to which is the real town, as those who tried to book in at the 'White Hart Hotel' (in reality the Stamford Arts Centre) discovered.[22] Enquiries from visitors as to when Middlemarch changed its name to Stamford may be in the minority, but perhaps reflect the playful way in which the history of the two towns has been juxtaposed.

However, central to the balance between the fake and the real is the issue of authenticity; yet this does not seem of great importance to the visitor. This lack of concern is recognised by Umberto Eco, who suggests in *Travels in Hyperreality* that there is a more casual attitude towards the problem of authenticity in present society: 'Everything looks real, and therefore it is real; in any case the fact that it seems real is real, and the thing is real even if, like Alice in Wonderland, it never existed.'[23] For the tourist, the Georgian buildings themselves are the object of the 'tourist's gaze' because of their authenticity.[24] Overall the contrivance of Stamford as Middlemarch problematises the distinction between authenticity and fake: a postmodern experience which is fundamental in creating nostalgia. Furthermore it sets an agenda for a range of production and consumption relationships which are central in the intertextual consumption of nostalgia.

The recent growth in the popularity of museums and heritage spectacles has been well documented by Lowenthal, Hewison, Urry and Merriman.[25] Whilst more leisure time and a growth in disposable incomes have contributed to the increase in demand for tourist experiences, changes in media consumption raise expectations of those experiences. As John Urry argues, the impact of wider and more visual media consumption is likely to encourage consumers to widen their gaze away from the more ordinary tourist activities towards the more extra-ordinary.[26] This has resulted in increased consumption of special interest activities such as customised weekend breaks. There is an intertextuality of consumption as listeners and viewers are encouraged to read *Doris Archer's Diary*, visit Ambridge or take specialist George Eliot and *Middlemarch* weekend breaks at the Hilton National East Midlands.[27] In each of these cases consumers are likely to be drawn from a population of fans or enthusiasts. Our analysis now focuses on the consumers of the Stamford-Middlemarch experiences.

Both official and unofficial sources indicate evidence of a clear, if fragmented, 'Middlemarch effect' on the tourist industry at Stamford. Official museum records show that the numbers of visitors and associated contacts more than doubled between 1992/3 (12,345) and 1994/5 (25,650) with a small but perceptible increase in international tourists, mainly from the US and Australia.[28] An increase in demand for Blue Badge guided tours is reported, especially in 1994, although no formal records exist.[29] In addition, reports from traders suggest that there has been an increase in visitors to the town because of the *Middlemarch* connection. The duty manager at the George Hotel, a major hotel in Stamford, told us that as a direct result of *Middlemarch* the hotel caters for an increase in guests from Britain and the US.[30]

Research on the heritage industry, of which Stamford-Middlemarch is one example, has tended to concentrate on the producers rather than the consumers. Where consumers have been surveyed some researchers, for example Greene, Griggs and Hays-Jackson, are more concerned with consumer perceptions than social class constituencies.[31] Those who have investigated the backgrounds of consumers (Heady, Moore, Merriman) conclude that higher status groups and those with tertiary education predominate.[32] Merriman's research, drawing on the work of Bourdieu and Goldthorpe *et al.*, is a variation on the embourgeoisement thesis, this time applied to leisure.[33] Merriman argues that the relatively affluent may be using their leisure to increase their cultural capital as a way of promoting their chances of upward social mobility.[34] Our observation of a tour of Stamford indicated a predominance of women over men, in a generally middle-class and middle-aged sample. This has been confirmed as typical of such tours and provides some indication that the constituencies of visitors to Stamford resemble other heritage users.[35]

The significance of cultural or intellectual capital, as an alternative to economic capital, has been identified by Bourdieu as an important factor in terms of educational advancement.[36] Knowing how to engage with the dominant codes in literature, art or philosophy enhances cultural competences and facilitates access to a privileged status not dependent on economic status.

Postwar Britain has been characterised by changes in the class structure which include a growth in the service class. Although this is not an undifferentiated, homogeneous group in economic terms, many of the economic indices (for example, job security, home and share ownership) which would have provided measures of difference in the past have been eroded. As a consequence, cultural capital becomes an important differentiating factor. Lee puts this clearly when he says:

since the second world war [as there has been] a genuine effacement of many of the economic differences by which class distinctions have traditionally been signalled, then questions of culture and cultural difference become paramount to our understanding of the manner in which hegemony and social order are both maintained and reproduced.[37]

The openness and accessibility of museums and heritage sites are identified by Merriman as providing opportunities for the service class to enhance their cultural capital.[38] Unlike other institutions such as societies and clubs, they are relatively cheap and do not rely on sponsorship. At Stamford it is possible to purchase the town trail and postcards of the filming for less than £3, tour Stamford with a Blue Badge Guide or enjoy a museum talk for around £2. Further, as Kevin Walsh argues, one way that the growing service class acquires cultural capital is through the 'traditionally English' method of 'integration through participation'.[39] The TV representation of *Middlemarch* and the opportunities to 'gaze upon the historical set for real' can facilitate the development of such capital.[40] Access to cultural capital and acquisition of cultural competence by the service class can be seen as one way in which cultural difference can be maintained and reproduced.

Middlemarch on TV is just one example of the way in which high culture is being transformed for a wider, mass audience. The distinctive feature of the transformation of *Middlemarch* is the Stamford connection, which goes beyond the TV series and draws on our nostalgic images of Britain's past. To visit Stamford is not to visit Middlemarch, although some consumables playfully challenge this divide. It is one way in which our cultural heritage is presented for consumers who are looking for more security in an insecure present. Post-Fordist commodification of experience is potentially renewable, although there may be limits as to how often tourists would be willing to do the town trail at Stamford. The Stamford experience is typical of postmodern culture in that it engages the audience with the cultural object. The representation of that object and the relationship with the audience are key features of the nostalgic debate.

Visitors to Stamford are presented with a sanitised representation of our cultural heritage insofar as they do not gaze on the impoverished and the politically weak. A similar point is made by Bob West in a penetrating critique of the heritagisation of Blists Hill at the Ironbridge Gorge Museum.[41] There is a particular irony in this heritagisation of Stamford, given that one of the main characters of the book, Dorothea, cultivates a role as a public benefactor. Are such visitors aware of the selective representations? Clearly there is more work to be done here but our case study suggests that there is a critical and sometimes challenging dimension to the presentation of history. Tourists are not merely passive consumers unaware of the divisions between the authentic and the fake, the rich and the poor and the gender divide. They are, however, likely to be encouraged to challenge these ideas further by a more politically sensitive portrayal by the nostalgia industry.

Nostalgia: is it what it used to be? Nicholas Zurbrugg categorises the final phase of postmodernism into 'Prophetic Pessimism' and 'Prophetic Optimism'.[42] He suggests that there is an optimism to be found in the creativity of such post-modernist multimedia artists as Laurie Anderson who, nevertheless, in her recent album *Bright Red* asks the question, 'And what I really want to know is: are things getting better or are they getting worse?'.[43] Theorists of the consumption of nostalgia are divided on the answer. Whilst some see the consumption of nostalgia as a feature of an economy in decline,[44] Hewison, in fact, goes further and argues that nostalgia neuters history and separates it from the present so that 'The true product of the heritage industry is not identity and security, but entropy. If history is over, then there is nothing to be done.'[45] Hewison, then, in some ways sees things getting worse, with nostalgia contributing to this decline. The construction and consumption of nostalgia serves to divert attention from the present, thereby preventing any critical appraisal.

There are some tensions here when compared with the view postulated by Walsh who points to the ways that the emergent service class may use the consumption of nostalgia to acquire cultural capital.[46] An active, engaged audience of the type we have observed consuming Middlemarch contributes to this process. This can be seen as part of a democratising hegemonic struggle to gain cultural competence and cultural capital. It suggests at least a dynamic which challenges the stasis of earlier theorists. Things may not be better but they have the potential to be so.

Notes

1. Kathleen Adams, *George Eliot: A Brief Biography* (Coventry: The George Eliot Fellowship, 1994) p. 19.
2. Broadcasters' Audience Research Board (BARB) 1994.
3. John Smith, Curator Stamford Museum, interview with authors, 5 June 1995.
4. Louis Marks in Stamford Museum Leaflet, Lincolnshire County Council.
5. J.B. Sykes, *The Concise Oxford Dictionary*, 6th edn (Oxford: Oxford University Press, 1976), p. 744.
6. Robert Hewison, *The Heritage Industry: Britain in a Climate of Decline* (London: Methuen, 1987), p. 46.
7. Michael Wood, 'Nostalgia or never: you can't go home again', *New Society*, 30, 631 (November 1974), pp. 343–6; Hewison, *The Heritage Industry*, p. 46, and Sir Roy Strong quoted in Hewison, p. 46.
8. Martyn J. Lee, *Consumer Culture Reborn* (London, New York, Canada: Routledge, 1993), p. 165.
9. John Urry, *The Tourist Gaze* (London, California, New Delhi: Sage, 1990), pp. 84–5, who notes his indebtedness to Scott Lash, *Sociology of Postmodernism* (London: Routledge, 1990).
10. *Guardian*, 12 April 1995.
11. Ibid.

12. Rob Shields (ed.), *Lifestyle Shopping, The Subject of Consumption* (London: Routledge, 1992), p. 2, who acknowledges M. de Certeau, *The Practice of Everyday Life* (Berkeley: University of California Press, 1984).
13. Urry, *The Tourist Gaze*, p. 85.
14. BBC Marketing Dept., June 1995.
15. Gerry Scott's interview is recorded by C. Bazalgette and C. James (eds), *Screening Middlemarch: C19th Novel to 90's Television* (BBC Education Pack in association with BFI, 1994).
16. A video for media studies has been produced by Bazalgette and James, *Screening Middlemarch* and the unofficial video *Middlemarch and Stamford* was shown at the Stamford Museum's exhibition of the filming of Middlemarch, 18 April–19 June 1994.
17. Advertisement in *Stamford & Middlemarch, A Rutland and Stamford Mercury Souvenir*, p. 24, and interview with the owners of Bombay Brasserie by the authors, 25 May 1995.
18. David Harvey, *The Condition of Postmodernity* (Oxford: Blackwell, 1989), p. 85.
19. Owner of Black Orchid dress shop, interview with authors, 25 May 1995.
20. Lee, *Consumer Culture*, p. 135.
21. John Smith, Curator Stamford Museum, interview with authors, 5 June 1995.
22. Jill Collinge, Blue Badge Guide, 22 June 1995.
23. Umberto Eco, *Travels in Hyperreality* (London: Picador, 1987), p. 16.
24. Urry, *Tourist Gaze*, p. 120.
25. David Lowenthal, *The Past is a Foreign Country* (Cambridge: Cambridge University Press, 1985), p. 4; Hewison, *Heritage Industry*, p. 9; Robert Hewison, 'The heritage industry revisited', *Museums Journal*, 91, 4 (April 1991), pp. 23–6; Urry, *Tourist Gaze*, p. 104; Nicholas Merriman, *Beyond the Glass Case* (Leicester: Leicester University Press, 1991), p. 92.
26. Urry, *Tourist Gaze*, pp. 101–2.
27. Jock Gallagher, *Doris Archer's Diary* (London: BBC, 1971); George Eliot and *Middlemarch* breaks are part of the Hilton National Hotel Chain's Special Interest Weekends.

28. Information supplied by John Smith, Curator Stamford Museum, May/June 1995 interviewed by the authors. Whilst no official records exist, museum staff and the tourist office note an increase in international visitors linked to the worldwide distribution of the TV series.
29. Jill Collinge, Blue Badge Guide, interview with authors, 22 June 1995.
30. Olf Ortmann, Duty Manager, The George Hotel, Stamford, 25 May 1995.
31. J.P. Greene, 'A visitor survey at Norton Priory Museum', *Museums Journal* 78, 1 (June 1978), pp. 7–9; S.A. Griggs and K. Hays-Jackson, 'Visitors' perceptions of cultural institutions', *Museums Journal* 83, 2/3 (Sept./Dec. 1983), pp. 121–5.
32. P. Heady, *Visiting Museums* (London: HMSO, 1984), pp. 12–20; R. Moore, 'Research Surveys', *Museums Journal* 88, 3 (December 1988), pp. 119–23; Merriman, *Glass Case*, p. 171.
33. Merriman, *Glass Case*, p. 93; P. Bourdieu, *Distinction* (London: Routledge and Kegan Paul, 1984); J. Goldthorpe *et al.*, *The Affluent Worker in the Class Structure* (Cambridge: Cambridge University Press, 1969).
34. Merriman, *Glass Case*, p. 93.
35. Authors' case study based on Blue Badge guided tour, 22 June 1995.
36. Pierre Bourdieu, *Distinction*, trans. Richard Nice (London: Routledge, 1992), p. 2; R. Bocock and K. Thompson, *Social and Cultural Forms of Modernity* (Oxford: Polity Press, 1992) pp. 146–8.
37. Lee, *Consumer Culture*, p. 34.
38. Merriman, *Glass Case*, p. 131.
39. Kevin Walsh, *The Representation of the Past: Museums and Heritage in the Post-Modern World* (London: Routledge, 1992), p. 126.
40. Ibid., p. 118.
41. Bob West, 'The making of the English working past: a critical view of the Ironbridge Gorge Museum', in Robert Lumley (ed.), *The Museum-Time Machine* (New York: Routledge, 1988), pp. 36–62.

42. Nicholas Zurbrugg, *The Parameters of Postmodernism* (London: Routledge, 1993), pp. 163–5.
43. Laurie Anderson, *Bright Red* (New York: Warner Brothers, 1994).
44. Hewison, 'Heritage Industry Revisited', p. 23.
45. Hewison, *Heritage Industry*, p. 187.
46. Walsh, *Representation of Past*, Ch. 7.

7

Pleasure and Interpretation: Film Adaptations of Angela Carter's Fiction

Catherine Neale

The starting-point of this chapter is the reception of Angela Carter's work in literary and cultural criticism, much of which has been feminist in approach. In both respects – that of criticism on Carter and that of feminist analysis – there are gaps and silences. It is widely known that a considerable amount of research on Carter is in progress, and the amount of published criticism is growing. But Carter has so far been the subject of a limited range of articles and chapters, and it is fairly easy to gain a sense of their general drift. An understandable element of hagiography has crept in since her death in 1992. More generally, probably because of her impressive range of reference, her sheer intelligence and humour, and her characteristic stance as 'demythologiser' providing her with the role of critic as well as creator, Carter receives sympathetic explication, commentary and contextualisation. What her work does not receive, it seems, is that element of critique that might examine the implications and potential contradictions of her projects, or place her work within a framework that is not dictated by Carter herself. This raises a very broad question of the nature of critique, particularly in respect of contemporary writing. More specifically, however, the absence of an explicit theoretical stance on the part of many of Carter's critics indicates the struggle that feminist criticism in particular has to identify a methodology.

One area of Carter's work is an exception: her depiction and treatment of sexuality. Patricia Duncker's article on *The Bloody Chamber* remains a significant point of dialogue with Carter's assumptions, and takes a clear line in stating a particular feminist point of view that cannot agree with Carter's resolutions.[1]

This chapter in fact takes a generally traditional line in drawing on Carter's work to identify an area where there appear to be tensions. The exercise is exacerbated, however, by another aspect challenging to the critic: the power and ubiquitousness of Carter's own commentary on her work, in interviews, occasional essays and television programmes. These prove virtually impossible to sidestep, providing as they do a number of suggestive ways of approaching her texts, and never conveying a sense of coy or mischievous misdirection. Carter refuses any distinction between the critical and the creative, and with her, commentary and fiction exist on a continuum ('narrative is an argument stated in fictional terms'[2]), so that the critic can, quite reasonably, accord authority to her statements. If one has lingering doubts about trusting the teller, Lorna Sage takes some trouble to define Carter's evolving construction of her role as writer and performer, culminating in what Sage calls 'the proliferation, rather than the death, of the author'.[3] Indeed, Sage's monograph clarifies another apparent contradiction: Carter's celebration of the anonymity and collective ownership of folk tales and her increasingly public profile through which she capitalised on the individualist opportunities available to the writer in the marketplace in contemporary times, even after her death.[4] Nevertheless, for the student of Carter there remains a methodological challenge in Carter's authorship and authority, especially in relation to her collaborative work on the film adaptations of her work, and the issue of intention.

With the theme of this collection in mind, it seems that there are a number of fruitful boundaries being questioned that are apposite to Carter. False distinctions between literature and film, and between high culture and popular culture, are the topic of much of her work:

> I think I must have started very early on to regard the whole of western European culture as a kind of folklore. I had a perfectly regular education, and indeed I'm a rather booksy person, but I do tend to regard all aspects of culture as coming in on the same level.[5]

The ironies of this point of view when considered alongside her own published work – the loss of collective storytelling, the intellectual self-consciousness that replaces a common culture – are recognised by Carter in *Nights at the Circus* in particular. For all of Carter's work is suffused with the self-consciousness of twentieth-century knowledge. It is not possible, as her fiction makes clear, to dream and to enjoy without interpretation. Her novels combine storytelling, argument and analysis in a way that places great demands on the reader, and that has several results in criticism of her work. There is an attempt to categorise her work, and thereby defuse it, by explaining it to be 'postmodernist' or 'magic realist' or 'surreal'. There are attempts to respond to her ideas by relating them to other paradigms, which I have suggested is Duncker's approach. There are excited and even flattered understandings of her books, in which an educated enjoyment is implicit. Carter seems to have succeeded in combining the illusion and magic of storytelling with self-consciousness for many of her readers.

Yet the case of the two films associated with her, adaptations of parts of *The Bloody Chamber* and of the novel *The Magic Toyshop*, raises questions about the shift from writing to image, from literature to film. Given Carter's engagement with cinema, and her identification of it as the predominant twentieth-century mode of collective pleasure (with all its inherent equivocations), her own films emerge as curiously downbeat hybrids. The important storytelling voices in Carter's fiction work to create a sense of a listening audience despite the privacy of the printed word, but the cinema remains a public and shared experience. The representation and reception of visual images are controversial for many engaged in cultural studies precisely because of their public identity, independent of an author. In addition, the technology of film allows for a range of effects and interpretations that pass beyond an essentially literary attention to narrative or argument within film.

'A critique of the Hollywood movie is a critique of the imagination of the twentieth century in the West', writes Carter in a review of Robert Coover's *A Night at the Movies*, and she identifies 'the magnificent gesticulations of giant forms, the bewildering transformations, the orgiastic violence that hurts nobody because it is not real' as 'all the devices of dream, or film, or fiction'.[6] In a subsequent review she stresses the marketplace of Hollywood, but concludes: 'The hell of it was, they made wonderful movies, then, when nothing in Hollywood was real except hard work, mass production, the conveyor belt, the tyrants, and madmen running the studios.'[7] In *Wise Children*, Carter conducts a simultaneous deconstruction and celebration of Hollywood in her depiction of a film version of *A Midsummer Night's Dream*: the film is the culmination of all Carter's ideas which favour the illegitimacies of popular culture; and the cultural icon of Shakespeare, of course, is both reduced and reinstated. In this, her final novel, Carter sets forth a determinedly optimistic view of the unofficial and its inevitable collusion with capitalism. She was less forgiving in 1977, in *The Passion of New Eve*. In that novel, the toils of ideology and of gender construction are attributed to Hollywood, and the alternatives offered are an equally problematic mythological past and a utopian notion of a new future.

For Carter, then, film, like dream or fiction, contains the possibilities for images to move through narrative in endless transformations. The 'movie' is the space of this illusion – which is also real – and the term itself evokes the glamour of Hollywood. In turn, Hollywood comes to represent the twentieth-century admixture of commercialism, exploitation and magic, and cinema signifies not only the film but the place of communal pleasure.

We should place these notions within a larger concern, in Carter's work, with the nineteenth and twentieth-century arenas of communal pleasure. After the storytelling circle, there remain the circus, the fairground, the music hall, and the cinema, all bearing strong associations with late nineteenth-century culture. Frequently these are contrasted with the high culture of opera (*The Bloody Chamber*) and with literature, by means of pervasive allusion.

Despite her wry acknowledgement that entertainment must now always be paid for (Uncle Philip in *The Magic Toyshop* abruptly reminds his niece of the economics of toymaking and business), Carter retains a utopian streak. This is often represented by her through reflections on the 1960s, and centres on her most controversial explorations into the nature of (hetero)sexuality. While she states in *The Sadeian Woman* that sexuality is possibly the least natural and most constructed of human activities, she nevertheless proposes that it offers a significant possibility for freedoms. Similarly, pleasure can be snatched from the jaws of exploitation and control.

Laura Mulvey begins an essay on Carter's cinema by stressing the possibilities for transformation and metamorphosis in the moving picture. Carter's writing, she says, features transformation so often that 'her books seem to be pervaded by this magic cinematic attribute even when the cinema itself is not present on the page'.[8] She notes that Freud was working on *The Interpretation of Dreams* during the same decade that cinema was developed. Mulvey emphasises Freud's habit of interpretation, but equally significant is Freud's description of the ability of dream-images to transform themselves: this, along with Freud's rational faith in interpretation, is the basis of Carter's equation of dream, narrative, film and fiction.

Both films, when viewed critically, are characteristic of Carter's approach. *The Company of Wolves*, which was released in 1984 and distributed beyond the art-house circuit, was co-scripted by Carter and Neil Jordan, and based on Carter's written work. Its concentric narrative structure, lurid colours and general lack of realist devices announce it as a defamiliarising film, and it combines storytelling with an exploration of the stories' implicit meanings. Carter scripted the 1988 film adaptation of *The Magic Toyshop*; the film bears manifest indications of Carter's desire for defamiliarisation. Here, it is achieved through abrupt cutting, and through the stilted performances of the actors, who thereby underline the equation of the puppets with the humans. There is consequently little developed characterisation, and Tom Bell's performance as Uncle Philip provides a semi-demented and alienating focus for the evident commentary on power and ideology. In both films there is congruence between Carter's themes, her commentary on those themes, and the translation of images on the screen. For example, the published book of *The Bloody Chamber* (from which the film *The Company of Wolves* is drawn) proposes that the distinction that western culture makes between human beings and animals is a false one; indeed, the narratives imply that animals' instinctive behaviour is nobler than the self-interest and materialistic urges of humans, and that humans have lost their impulses. This enables the film to envision numerous transformations between wolves and humans. In the novel of *The Magic Toyshop* Carter constructs another site of pleasure, the toyshop, which depends on commercialism. Within that, the toymaker, Uncle Philip, constructs puppets to act out scenarios on his private stage with the human beings within his power: scenarios of power and exploitation. Carter's equation of humans' need for toys to play with and the wilful dehumanisation of oppressed people is uncomfortable. Once again the film provides a valuable visual dimension in its depiction of Uncle Philip's performances, which self-consciously also draw the viewer into the position of manipulator, player, and voyeur.

Both films also create vivid images which require the viewer to engage in interpretation. Discussing *The Company of Wolves*, John Collick makes a useful point when he observes:

> The film constructs an elaborate framework of these, and other symbols. The problem with this web of signification is that it actually signifies very little, other than a string of familiar metaphors. What is being offered appears to be a parody of the Freudian dream work in which the dream symbols, instead of being scrambled images or 'puzzles' that represent unconscious wishes, turn out to be familiar literary images.[9]

What Collick identifies here as deliberate parody in fact occurs frequently in Carter's work, where over-signification leads the reader or viewer into a self-conscious distancing from their acts of interpretation. The films, like Carter's writings, combine illusion, seduction, interpretation and reflexivity. Collick's description of the films' symbols as 'familiar literary images', however, betrays the provenance of the films in the printed word.

There are two points in *The Company of Wolves* where the projects of seduction and defamiliarisation collide. A young girl gatecrashes an aristocratic wedding feast and her denunciation precipitates the transformation of the diners into wolves; in the ending to the film, the dreaming girl awakens to the wolves which burst through the window. These instances, dealt with in quite different technical ways, pose questions about the relationship between literature and film, in terms of their possible reception, and the possibilities and constraints that film specifically offers.

When the decadent aristos are metamorphosed into wolves, the echoes of Spencer Tracy's transformation in the 1941 film adaptation of *Dr Jekyll and Mr Hyde*, overlaid with a subsequent materialist analysis, are clear. What is less straightforward is how far the layers of historical reference can coexist with a viewing position that will respond to illusion. How can we simultaneously enjoy the illusion and register the references, without also registering laughable special effects, so deliberately out-of-date that they fail to convince? Mulvey describes *The Company of Wolves* as

> moving through a young girl's contemporary appropriation of the story for her own interior psychic needs to the social setting of oral culture, and then to the exteriorisation of the irrational in the ancient belief in monsters. In the cinema, worlds can open up and shift from one to another without verbal explanation. The cinema creates links and cross-references that share the imprecision manifested by the workings of the mind or the tangled displacements of collective fantasy.[10]

We are dealing here with a description of the possibilities of cinema, and an understanding of Carter's project, that are not tested against the celluloid artifact. The artifact remains crucial because it remains for Carter a locus of pleasure, visual and communal. Carter's emphasis on the material and physical constraints on film-making only accentuate the power of cinema to overcome them through fantasy and illusion. In the decision to sacrifice the illusion of transformation at this point in the film, presumably in order to force the viewer to appraise what they are seeing, elements of bathos and banality cannot be controlled.

In the case of the ending of the film, which is shot in a more transparently contemporary way, the benefits of such illusory realism paradoxically collide with the practical constraints of film. Carter's own commentary is a starting-point:

> The reason why the girl is pounced on by the wolves at the end is pure contingency, since the original ending that Neil wanted turned out to be impossible, literally not possible. He said that it must end on an 'extraordinary image' – an image of repression being liberated by libido – in which the girl would wake up and do the most beautiful dive into the floorboards ... there didn't seem to be any point in writing things he didn't want to film. In the final analysis any film is the director's movie. But the impossible remains impossible.[11]

Although Carter distances herself from authorship of the film here (while stating and reiterating her support for the film during the interview), the admission of the impossible places a constraint on the film that does not exist in the fiction. (Animation would have delivered the desired illusion, but would of course have undercut the aim of illusion within realism; this heretical reflection, however, serves to remind me of the essentially cerebral project within the film.)

In a discussion of the same sequence, John Collick describes three types of dreamfilms: those which present the viewer with dream imagery and cast the viewer as an analyst who will interpret the hidden meaning; those which replicate the experience of dreaming, unsettling the viewer's expectations of realism and narrative coherence; and those which interrogate Freudian frameworks and ultimately throw the viewer's own position into question. He argues that *The Company of Wolves* presents an apparent example of the first category, but that the conclusion promotes it to the third:

> the image makes explicit what has been implicit throughout the movie: that writing, filming and watching dreams (using the traditional Freudian methods of analysis to 'control' the unconscious) involve the adoption of inadequate and false positions of scientific objectivity ... A false, liberal and comforting conclusion is offered, and then effaced by the shot of the wolf bursting through the glass (which parallels

the destruction of the audience's position of authority as the incomprehensible meaning of the film 'bursts' through the screen).[12]

Any quibble that Collick makes a great deal out of a sequence that Carter implies was a concession to practical impossibility is only superficial: he has responded to the intention to present an 'extraordinary image'. Collick makes it clear that he is interested in dream films that are derived from texts, thus complying with Carter's implicitly literary approach to film. What is absent here is a consideration of how far the image (by its moving nature, both transient and irrecoverable for the viewer) can unite pleasure and defamiliarisation within the viewer.

Discussing the film of *The Magic Toyshop*, Laura Mulvey comments on the use of special effects:

> As Finn rehearses Melanie for her role as Leda, the cinema transforms his room into a wave-swept beach, where he can tell her his feelings and his determination to rebel. In Melanie's dream, the rose-coloured wallpaper of her room is turned into a rose garden, and the sad antlers nailed to the wall turn Finn into a faun.[13]

Here, film is effecting those transformations that for Carter both reflect the experience of dream and offer promises of liberation. Yet Mulvey herself goes on to betray that the film only assumes a role towards the end:

> [it] becomes freer in its use of cinema, with camera pans and tracks. It is as though the cinema's power to dream participates in the characters' assertion of their own desires and, at the same time, materialises them magically on the screen.[14]

This equivocal role of film, whereby it is made use of, but its distinctive possibilities only emerge, indicates again the literary angle from which both *The Company of Wolves* and *The Magic Toyshop* were made.

Angela Carter's strengths and interests lay in the sphere of the written word, and not in the extensive features of film.

The film adaptations of her writing seem particularly apposite because of her insistent fondness for the cinema. However, they remain adaptations, a part of the way in which many literary texts have been adopted for filmic representation. Carter herself may not have been disconcerted by this observation: after all, Hollywood's adaptation of *A Midsummer Night's Dream* is a central event in *Wise Children*, and comes to signify the translation of pleasure from one medium to another in the course of history. Nevertheless, the magical transformation of images, reflecting the workings of dream and the survival of illusion, when made possible by the technical advancement of film, undercuts the essentially literal and literate analysis of such illusion. There are differences of audience, of context and of technical circumstance that Carter may have wished to break down, but that also participate, ironically, in her version of twentieth-century culture.

Notes

1. Patricia Duncker, 'Re-imagining the fairy tales: Angela Carter's bloody chambers', *Literature and History* 10, 1 (1984), pp. 3–14.
2. Angela Carter, *Come unto these Yellow Sands: Four Radio Plays* (Newcastle upon Tyne: Bloodaxe Books, 1985), p. 7.
3. Lorna Sage, *Angela Carter* (Plymouth: Northcote House Publishers, 1994), p. 58.
4. Her literary executor writes that anything was to be done '"to make money for my boys" – her husband Mark and son Alexander. No vulgarity was to be spared; any one of her fifteen books could be set to music or acted on ice'; Susannah Clapp, Introduction to Angela Carter, *American Ghosts and Old World Wonders* (London: Chatto and Windus, 1993), p. ix.
5. John Haffenden, *Novelists in Interview* (London: Methuen, 1985), p. 85.
6. Angela Carter, *Expletives Deleted: Selected Writings* (London: Chatto and Windus, 1992), pp. 131, 132.
7. Carter, *Expletives Deleted*, p. 137.
8. Laura Mulvey, 'Cinema magic and the old monsters: Angela Carter's cinema', in Lorna Sage (ed.) *Flesh and the*

Mirror: Essays on the Art of Angela Carter (London: Virago, 1994), p. 230.

9. John Collick, 'Wolves through the window: writing dreams/dreaming films/filming dreams', *Critical Survey* 3, 3 (1991), p. 286.
10. Mulvey, 'Cinema magic and the old monsters', pp. 239–40.
11. Haffenden, *Novelists in Interview*, pp. 84–5.
12. Collick, 'Wolves through the window', p. 286.
13. Mulvey, 'Cinema magic and the old monsters', p. 237.
14. Ibid., p. 237.

8

Capitalism Most Triumphant: Bill & Ted's Excellent History Lesson

I.Q. Hunter

Since the late 1980s an important new mini-genre has emerged in American films: the Dumb White Guy movie. Owing a little, perhaps, to Jerry Lewis and the Three Stooges and rather more to anarchic gross-out comedies like *Porky's* and *National Lampoon's Animal House*, films such as *Wayne's World*, *Forrest Gump*, *Dumb and Dumber*, *Airheads* and the TV show *Beavis and Butthead* glorify the Dumb White Guy as an all-American cultural hero. Apparently endorsing the cliché that, driven remorselessly downward by TV, American popular culture is becoming ever more stupid, hedonistic and anti-social, these movies celebrate the virtues of dumbness, slacking and trash culture, either as cynical escapes from responsibility or as styles of incoherent revenge against respectability, intellectualism and the horrors of political correctness.

At least that is one popular interpretation, vigorously expressed by pundits in the quality press. Another reading is possible, however. In my view, the films are neither lurid symptoms of anomie and cultural degeneration, nor, as squeamish liberals might insist, boorish manifestations of a white male backlash. Instead I see them as working through the cultural contradictions of what Francis Fukuyama notoriously called 'the end of history': the simultaneous triumphs of consumer capitalism and American popular culture. Fukuyama's 1989 essay 'The end of history?' and his subsequent book *The End of History and the Last Man*, argued, somewhat prematurely as it turned out, that with the collapse of communism, a certain kind of utopia had arrived, in the sense that no further ideological development was possible.[1]

111

Drawing on a curious amalgam of ideas, from Plato to Hegel to Kojève, and reworking the 'end of ideology' thesis of the 1950s, Fukuyama claimed that consumer capitalism would from now on be the model for human aspiration. There were several reasons for this: the most important for our purposes is that capitalism offered dreams that money can buy, its triumph representing what Fukuyama called 'the victory of the VCR' – the utopian appeal of consumerist plenty.[2]

Fukuyama's historicist triumphalism was, however, sharply modified by a sense of the banality, triviality and boredom to which consumerism seemed thereby to condemn the future. Fukuyama was concerned that consumers 'risk becoming secure and self-absorbed' with no interest in 'striving for higher goals in our pursuit of private comforts', with subsequent damage both to a sense of community and to the puritan ethic necessary for capitalism to flourish.[3] By a fine paradox, the capitalist utopia achieved in the US and dreamt about everywhere else was turning out to be unbearably banal, trashy, relativistic and – more predictable, perhaps – selfishly materialist. Not only, as Krishan Kumar remarks, might it undermine 'the sense of solidarity and community' but it 'might bore us to death, in its lack of challenge to our more active faculties'.[4] Still, as Kumar goes on to say, 'If only this were all! For if so, most of us might settle for a quiet private life of comfort and consumption, and let those who want to worry about the higher things of the mind.'[5]

This well-appointed utopia nurtures what Fukuyama calls, following Nietzsche, 'Last Men', who, lacking religious or philosophical props, crave nothing else than leisure, material pleasures and a nice, easy-going 'lifestyle'. Laid-back and unheroic, snugly cocooned from romantic yearnings and existential shocks, these Last Men represent 'the victory of "sloth", the nihilistic sense that there can be nothing worth seriously affirming or negating'.[6] As Dennis Cooper notes, commentators have 'variously identified [the Last Man] with the self-satisfied, convention-bound bourgeois salaud; the faceless product of what Mill called "rational socialist" society; the zombies of Orwell's and Huxley's allegories; or the dully contented hedonist, the "pig satisfied"'.[7] Cooper, perturbed that capitalism has itself become the main engine of individualistic pluralism, argues – I think disingenuously – that the morality of the Last Man is really

> manifested in the 'laid back' attitude of young people, including those students upon whose relativism, according to Allan Bloom, professors can today rely, [for whom] seeking one's pleasures and indulging one's preferences – now dignified as 'choice of lifestyle' or 'conception of the good life' – are elevated into 'human rights'.[8]

Dumb White Guys are the shock troops of the end of history, who benevolently further the spread of consumerism by trashing morality, high culture and taste. Culturally, they are in the avant-garde, their postmodern affectlessness promoting the pluralistic values of the Last Man. For if, as Fukuyama argued, the US is the economic model for any future society, its success appears necessarily to have come at the price of an amnesiac, hedonistic 'dumb' culture corrosive of hierarchies of taste and value. And it is this culture, the Dumb White culture of TV, Hollywood movies and rock music, which is becoming truly universal, having proved the most effective advertisement for the American utopia. As James Twitchell remarks, commenting on Fukuyama:

> What legitimizes [his] claim ['the eluctable spread of consumerist Western culture'] is that it is demonstrably true. For better or worse, American culture is already world culture. Certainly one of the unadvertised aspects of the New World Order is the dominance of world-wide conglomerated media and the effacement of culture-specific aesthetic categories like high art ... [It is] likely that the globalization of show business will result in the heroic materialism of an ever-increasing worldwide consumerist culture.[9]

This brings us back to the unfortunate contradiction between the high ideals of capitalism and marketplace realities. As it responds to the desires of the masses, consumerism is as amoral as it is democratic. Relativism, the upshot of all this, is very often identified with (and, for some reason, blamed on) the scary catch-all, 'postmodernism'. Relativism has inspired considerable anxiety among the likes of Allan Bloom, E.D. Hirsch and Gertrude Himmelfarb (echoed, though, by many on the Left), who are distressed by the uncoupling of consumer capitalism from traditional moral and cultural values. But such alarm at 'the vulgarisation of culture in postmodern America' (Twitchell's phrase) is merely the rage of Caliban seeing his own face – or rather the faces, to switch the cliché, of countless dumb white Frankenstein's monsters.[10] For – an obvious point – capitalism's triumph, splendid as it was, owed a great deal to the seductive vulgarity of consumerist popular culture, as well as to the irresistible appeal of becoming Last Men.

Bill & Ted's Excellent Adventure, directed in 1988 by Stephen Herek and one of the first of these 'dumb' films, is a witty account of these ambiguous implications of consumerist triumphalism. The setting is contemporary San Dimas, California where two 15 year olds, Bill S. Preston Esquire (Alex Winter) and Ted 'Theodore' Logan (Keanu Reeves), noted for their gormlessness and command of valley-speak idiolect, are threatened with failing a history exam. Rufus (George Carlin), from 700 years into the future, intervenes to prevent this by lending them his time-machine. Bill and Ted kidnap various historical figures, including Napoleon, Freud and Socrates, and put them in a rock-show-like presentation that enables them to pass the course. Bill and Ted are then free to form their rock band, Wyld Stallyns, and so bring about world peace and the survival of the planet. In the future, it seems, Bill and Ted are regarded as the 'great ones', whose music and ideas have become the basis for civilisation.

Despite generally poor or condescending critical reaction, *Bill & Ted's Excellent Adventure* did well enough at the box-office to ensure a sequel, *Bill & Ted's Bogus Journey* (1991), and franchised spin-offs such as a comic book and a cartoon TV series, *Bill & Ted's Excellent Adventures*, voiced by Reeves and Winter. The original film is now a cult item, not least because of its heroes' ritualised and creatively hyperbolic dialogue, a pastiche of surfer jargon and the valley girl-speak parodied in Frank Zappa's song 'Valley Girl'. In fact *Bill & Ted* is among an increasing number of ready-made cult movies, whose numerous references and in-jokes are specifically designed to encourage audience loyalty and lucrative repeat viewings.

Though a teen comedy, *Bill & Ted* is a droll satire of contemporary worries about the 'dumbing down' of popular
culture and of American teen culture in particular. Bill and Ted
are ignorant, steeped in mass culture, and lack all sense of
historical tradition. Julius Caesar, according to Bill, was a
'solid-dressing dude'; Napoleon a 'short, dead dude'; Joan of
Arc was probably Noah's wife. What little they do know
consists of clichés, quotations from pop culture and fragments
gleaned from unlikely sources: George Washington is the
'father of the country', 'the dollar bill guy ... born on President's
day' and – a significant reference – the dude in Disneyland's
Hall of Presidents. The film does well to focus on historical
ignorance, which is often regarded as one of the defining
qualities of our alleged postmodern malaise. From Bloomians
fearing the loss of the sustaining traditions of Western civilisation, to Marxists like Fredric Jameson who gloomily diagnose
the waning of historical sense, the charge is that, as Jim Collins
puts it, 'evil postmodern culture has "reduced" the world to
images that it then cannibalizes'.[11] In many ways *Bill & Ted*
underwrites these contemporary fears, not least by representing youth culture as terminally inane, trivialising and
self-absorbed. Yet the film's address to the audience is very far
from dumb. Though each of the main characters is a Dumb
White Guy, the implied addressees are surely not, if they are
to make sense of the film at all. *Bill & Ted* requires not only
skills of cine-literacy and ironic detachment (as indeed do all
postmodern films) but, more important, an assured, cynical
familiarity with current moral panics about consumerism,
teenagers and pop culture. (After all, doesn't *everyone* know that
American kids nowadays are stupid, badly educated and
obsessed by rock music and TV?) The film's postmodern
address short-circuits patronising accounts of popular culture,
accounts it gleefully incorporates in the forms of parody and
exaggeration.

Bill & Ted is a curiously hybridized teen-movie. It combines
elements of campus comedy (*Back to School, Fast Times at
Ridgemont High*) and science fiction (*Back to the Future I–III, Time
Bandits*) and even the old Bob Hope/Bing Crosby road movies,
but this gives little sense of the generic complexity afforded
by its time-travel conceit. (Most Hollywood films are

'hyphenates' these days, opportunistic fusions of successful formulae. Thus *Under Siege* is *Die Hard*-on-a-boat, *Waterworld* is *Mad Max*-on-water, and so on. *Bill & Ted* might be pitched along the lines of *Back to the Future*-meets-*Revenge of the Nerds*.) Individual scenes parody specific genres – the western, medieval movies, futuristic science fiction – but more often genericity is signified by glancing allusions to famous movies instead of by sustained pastiche. (The medieval sequence, for example, turns on a rescue scene imitating the Errol Flynn *Adventures of Robin Hood*.) This quickfire allusionism is taken even further in the sequel, whose channel-surfing approach to genre is virtually freeform, taking in the horror film (possession scenes inspired by *The Exorcist*), religious imagery (visits to Heaven and Hell) and the art film (Death appears, complete with Swedish accent, as in Bergman's *The Seventh Seal*; this is an all-purpose reference to European movies – he also turns up in *Last Action Hero*). The allusions are complicated by being not only movie-specific but also cross-referenced with heavy metal imagery. In *Bogus Journey*, for instance, God is found at the top of the stairway from *A Matter of Life and Death*. But this unlikely filmic quotation (like Death, it introduces 'art-house' allusions possibly unfamiliar to the intended audience) is also an unforced comic homage to Led Zeppelin: in the US Powell and Pressburger's film was retitled *Stairway to Heaven*. Hell, too, while owing something to Dante, owes rather more to representations on heavy metal album covers (though Bill is disconcerted that it does not precisely concur with them: 'We've been totally lied to by our album covers, man').

Reflexivity is usual in postmodern films. What is telling here is that Bill and Ted, as connoisseurs of the impertinent allusion, are entirely at home regardless of the location and historical period. Popular culture has conveniently recycled history into a series of theme-park locations and pleasurable restagings of old movies. Bill and Ted are delighted when a bar fight breaks out in the Old West simply because the past is acting in character ('This is just like Frontierland!'). When they kidnap Napoleon in 1805, they look across at his armies and see stock footage of *War and Peace*: the past is literally textualised. Popular culture offers a lingua franca by which Bill and Ted can negotiate any situation. Their mass cultural capital is surprisingly useful, offering a bathetic parallel for the most outlandish occasion. Socrates is compared with Ozzy Osbourne because both were 'accused of corrupting youth'; Bill and Ted woo the 'medieval babes' and philosophise with Socrates by quoting rock lyrics ('All we are is dust in the wind,' Ted declares, to Socrates' delight); in *Bogus Journey*, they already have the measure of Death – 'Don't fear the reaper', Bill says, taking his cue from Blue Oyster Cult.

The key metaphor for this absurd promiscuity of reference is the time-machine lent by Rufus, a telephone booth (presumably a nod to Dr Who's Tardis), which enables them to call up and 'bag' history. Bill and Ted, unthinking cultural imperialists, literalise postmodern culture's instant access to and eclectic appropriation of the past. They encounter only what Eco called anticipated quotations of simulated histories, reprocessed in their culture's own image. The result is a sophis-ticated and multi-levelled game with perceptions of the past, reflecting, in Jim Collins's words, 'not just the increasing sophistication of the cinematic literacy of ... audiences (and the profoundly intertextual nature of that literacy), but also the entertainment value that the ironic manipulation of that stored information now provides'.[12]

By calling the film 'postmodern', I don't mean that Herek necessarily intended it that way. Intention is certainly undervalued in current writing about film, but the knowing playfulness of texts like *Bill & Ted* is not really evidence of traffic between high and low culture, of Godardian tricks percolating downwards by the efforts of frustrated art-movie *auteurs*. To a large extent, popular culture simply *is* postmodernism: wilfully ironic, tricksily referential and permanently within quotation marks. For example, given that effects of ironic dis-tanciation are often regarded as signs of avant-garde intent, it is worth noting how frequently they turn up even in so-called exploitation films. *Scumbusters*, a little-known but represen-tative exploitation movie from 1988, 'warns' audiences of impending scenes of nudity and violence with, respectively, a 'hooter horn' and a 'gore gong'. Similarly, Fred Olen Ray's *Bad Girls from Mars* indulges in numerous comic asides to the audience, quirky metanarrational devices that serve to underline the genre's ridiculous conventions. In one scene, while characters decry the gratuitous nudity in 'this kind of film', a woman performs a striptease in the foreground. It is a perfectly judged 'deconstructive' moment.

This kind of knowing self-reference throws up problems for critical analyses, especially for determinedly symptomatic ones. A good example is that postmodern films tend to confuse text and subtext, to the point where critical disinterment of hidden or symptomatic meanings seems rather a wasted effort. *Scumbusters* and *Bad Girls from Mars* are not unusual in anticipating critical moves. *Bill & Ted*, for instance, is very knowing (or sardonic) about its Oedipal subtexts (signalled by the inclusion of Freud as a key historical figure). The viewer, drawing on some cultural capital, can easily work up a pop psychoanalytical reading of the film; indeed, we are actively encouraged to. Bill's stepmother is Missy, his contemporary and the source of much Oedipal confusion – Ted had once taken her out; Bill's father makes love to her in his son's bedroom; Bill needs frequently to be reminded that 'She's your stepmom, dude!' At the same time the film offers a series of oppressive, castrating fathers: Bill's, who possesses Missy; Ted's, who wants to send his son to Oates Military Academy; and the medieval babes', who threatens to encase Bill and Ted in an 'iron maiden' (a *vagina dentata*) and afterwards behead them. The plot is quite clearly about Bill and Ted's resolution of the Oedipal complex (Ted, at a key moment, *steals his father's keys*) and their induction into patriarchy by various 'good' father figures (Rufus, Lincoln, the other 'forefathers'). At the end, Bill and Ted become forefathers themselves, of a world based narcissistically around their creative efforts. I labour this obvious point not to suggest that crude psychoanalytic readings of the film are out of bounds to critics with nothing better to do – unfortunately they never are – but that, on the contrary, their possibility is teasingly foregrounded. The film's dollar-book Freudism is made explicit at the presentation, when Freud explains that Ted's father takes out his insecurities on his son. Bill shies away from analysis, explaining, to Missy's bafflement, that he's just got a minor Oedipal problem. The point, of course, is that postmodern popular culture recycles symptomatic interpretations along with everything else. The critic, in seeming to read deeply into a postmodern text, more often finds that it will always keep one step ahead.

The roll-call of historical figures kidnapped by Bill and Ted is a parodic reduction of Western Civ. Each stands for a period in history, visually represented by a clutch of movie references. Socrates embodies the ancient world, in other words sword-and-sandal movies; Billy the Kid, 'the western movement in America in the nineteenth century', in other words cowboy films. Each of the figures is reduced to an appropriately cartoonish compulsion: far from offering a cynical alternative view of San Dimas (as the Savage in *Brave New World* provides of modern civilisation), these great figures discover in its shopping mall, bowling alley and waterpark, a 'most unprecedented' leisure outlet for their special talents. They throw themselves overenthusiastically into the pleasures of postmodern culture, often misreading its simplest rules and conventions. Set loose in a shopping mall, Joan of Arc directs her energies into aerobics. Genghis Khan wrecks a sports store, dressed up in American football gear and wielding a baseball bat. Socrates, Freud and Billy the Kid cruise the local talent. Beethoven, who finds a synthesiser in a music shop, is so carried away with his new toy that he must be restrained by the police. Rufus introduces the 'medieval babes' to the delights of the mall and credit cards; they are instantly transformed into stereotypical Californian girls, as if that were indeed their true, natural state. Napoleon's all-devouring will to power is sublimated into mere greed for junk food: he wins a Ziggy-Piggy badge, having consumed a monstrous 'Ziggy Pig' ice-cream. His megalomaniac drives are further expended at the bowling alley and Waterloo, the local waterpark (the park's name is itself a brilliant metaphor not only of the culture's 'affectless' and levelling appropriation of great historical events but of violence transformed into harmless communal play). When each of these figures performs at Bill and Ted's presentation and passes judgement on San Dimas, the past is transformed into spectacle. The presentation is staged as a rock concert, but comes across, appropriately enough, as a theme-park reconstruction of history. The visitors wholly approve of San Dimas, having been inadvertently postmodernized by the experience. Beethoven's favourite music now includes both Mozart's Requiem and

Bon Jovi's *Slippery When Wet*, making comically irrelevant all distinctions between high and low culture. 'Socrates loves San Dimas' because it lives by his philosophy that 'true wisdom is to know that you know nothing'. (Postmodern relativism thus finds itself an ancient pedigree.) Joan of Arc decides to institute an aerobics regime for her soldiers on her return to France. Genghis Khan – 'that very excellent barbarian' – favours Twinkies for their high energy rush. And Napoleon, bagged in 1805 before his own Waterloo, is moved to include waterslides in his future battle-plans. The presentation builds to an address by Lincoln, who confirms the general enthusiasm for the state of modern consumerism. Reworking the Gettysburg Address, he offers a minimalist postmodern ethic 'as true today as it was in my time': 'Be excellent to each other – and party on, dudes!'

And so the past underwrites consumerism. *Bill & Ted* is equal to *Blade Runner* as a visualisation of the postmodern condition, its highly intertextual treatment of genres and allusions meshing with a vivid and coherent image of leisure culture. While *Blade Runner* is the canonical dystopian vision of postmodernity, Bill and Ted is its comically utopian counterpart, drawing on and parodying both the complacent ethnocentric boosterism of the Reagan years and its fears of cultural disintegration. Postmodernism (itself an apocalyptic subgenre of science fiction) has fewer utopias than dystopias, visualised – or rather allegorised by critics – in texts like *Blade Runner*, *RoboCop* and *Virtual Light*, where the future has collapsed into incomprehensible chaos. It is often said that postmodernism lends itself to spatial metaphors, usually urban or architectural: specific places which either represent the lived experience of postmodernism at its most acute or can be seen as futuristic incubators of globalising trends. The usual suspects are shopping malls and Disneyland; others include Las Vegas, the Pompidou Centre, the Bonaventure Hotel, the desert and the virtual realities of cyberspace. These, contrasting with the dystopian city (postmodern utopias tend to be suburban, nostalgic recreations of the past, or sealed off from urban reality), are zones of pleasure and consumption. Although descriptions of them are often more sarcastic than celebratory – one thinks of Eco on the 'degenerate utopia' of Disneyland

– they do invoke concrete postmodern utopias, founded on a recognition of contingency, diversity and desire.[13] As George Steiner put it, they embody the '"California promise" that the USA has offered to the common man on this tired earth. American standards of dress, nourishment, locomotion, entertainment, housing are today the concrete utopias in revolution.'[14] San Dimas is just such a place. The historical visitors become tourists (Bill acts as a tour guide in the mall, 'where people in today's world hang out'). They consume, windowshop and encounter spaces, such as Waterloo, entirely given over to mindless frivolity. The visitors fit in quite easily (no one, in this individualistic, easy-going paradise, blinks an eye at their historical fashions) and, naturally, they are won over. Yet, in the film's ironic perspective, it is uncertain whether San Dimas 1988 represents an easy, more or less frictionless life (for it is not entirely without problems: Napoleon gets thrown out of a bowling arcade for lack of money; exams are still to be passed, Military Academies to be avoided) or mindless submission to an infantilised and homogenised brave new world. For all its utopianism, the film does throw in fragments of other, more critical perspectives. We catch a glimpse, for example, of another student's presentation (interestingly, she is black), which refers to continuing class differences: the masses were once told to eat cake, she says, now they must watch TV.

The film therefore has an optimistic but distinctly ironic vision of historical progress. San Dimas 1988 is, strictly speaking, pre-utopian but contains all the elements of future perfection: leisure, an easy-going sense of community, and an unproblematic devotion to rock music and waterslides. Utopia itself, however, will only ever come about if Bill and Ted spread San Dimas's laid-back values globally through the music of Wyld Stallyns, 'putting an end to war and poverty, aligning the planets ... and leading to communication with aliens'. This ridiculous premise is more subtle than it appears; for all its unabashed Americanism, the film doesn't simply recycle Reaganite propaganda. As Stjepan Mestrovic has noticed, it shares the nervously apocalyptic tone of much *fin de siècle* popular culture. Its theme, albeit 'camouflaged in "fun" images', is, after all, the survival of civilisation itself.[15] *Bill & Ted* presents a comic but thoroughly contingent view of history, at once a parody of 'great man' theories (the 'great ones' here are two amiable idiots) and, more to the point, a cynical postmodern satire of historical metanarratives. Civilisation is very fragile in this film. The utopian society does not emerge because of historical necessity; its triumph is merely accidental and must be endlessly ensured by intervention from the future. History is always at risk of being set off course, rewritten and started up again.[16] The film admirably illustrates the postmodern view of history, disabused of Just So stories about inevitability and progress. As Stephen Jay Gould explains in *Wonderful Life*, the central principle of all history is indeed contingency.[17] From human evolution to the smallest occurrence, events might easily have been otherwise; the only rule is the cliché that the unexpected will usually happen. Long a mainstay of fiction, this principle has found unexpectedly powerful expression in recent popular films. Time-travel films such as *Back to the Future* (discussed by Gould) and *The Terminator* movies turn on the enormous consequences of the most trivial events – one mistake and history is, as it were, history. There is no underlying pattern, only the unintended consequences of ambiguously intended acts. *Bill & Ted*, no less 'chaotically', offers an apocalyptic vision of historical progress as contingent upon two idiots passing an examination.

The film's satirical utopianism is most apparent in the flash-forward to San Dimas 2700. Naturally, given the film's compulsive refererentiality, San Dimas 2700 is parodic of familiar modernist science fiction future states – all white domes, advanced but unobtrusive technology, and cleanliness (Rufus makes a point of this at the start of the film) – as well as conforming to more contemporary desires, being peaceful, multicultural, well-supplied with waterslides and founded on a universal popular culture. (*Bogus Journey*, in the visit to Heaven, offers an equivalent utopia, underlining this inter-pretation. Heaven, initially resembling a Holiday Inn, seems remarkably like San Dimas in 2700 – St Peter is black, God is benevolent and cool.) Thanks to Bill and Ted's peace-inducing music, the future is entirely rock-orientated. Its three elders are rock musicians, among them Clarence Clemons (Bruce Springsteen's saxophonist; he is black) and Fee Waybill of

The Tubes. This is a take-off (relevant in the wake of Live Aid) of popular music's imperialistic pretensions to cultural salvation. Rock magically resolves the problem of community: henceforth everyone will like the same music. But, ironically, this undermines the subversive appeal of rock music. It is no longer individualistic in the future but soulless, no longer diverse but an homogenised MOR, piped into the atmosphere like Muzak. In fact, although Rufus describes the future as 'great', the audience, cued by nagging allusions to other such science fiction futures (as in *Logan's Run* and *The Time Machine*), is likely to interpret it cynically as benevolent fascism. Everyone performs the same actions (the universal greeting is to play an air guitar), and dresses identically. The film's Dumb White Male fantasy – from which the audience, unlike Bill and Ted, is assumed to keep an ironic distance – ends with the elimination of all signs of difference. *Bill & Ted*'s key joke is that the supposed salvational music is white heavy metal, the most despised and unhip (and monocultural) of genres. The future is indeed a long revenge of the nerds.

Notes

1. Francis Fukuyama, 'The end of history?', *The National Interest* 16, pp. 3–18; Francis Fukuyama, *The End of History and the Last Man* (Harmondsworth: Penguin, 1992).
2. Fukuyama, *The End of History*, p. 98.
3. Ibid., p. 328.
4. Krishan Kumar and Stephan Bann, *Utopias and the Millenium* (London: Reaktion, 1993), p. 79.
5. Ibid., p. 79.
6. Dennis E. Cooper, 'Doing it my way – or your way', *Times Literary Supplement*, 27 April–3 May 1990, p. 444.
7. Ibid., p. 444.
8. Ibid., p. 444.
9. James B. Twitchell, *Carnival Culture: The Trashing of Taste in America* (New York: Columbia University Press, 1992), pp. 272–3.
10. Ibid., p. 253. See also Allan Bloom, *The Closing of the American Mind: How Higher Education Has Failed Democracy and Impoverished the Souls of Today's Students* (New York:

Simon & Schuster, 1987); E.D. Hirsch, Jr., *Cultural Literacy: What Every American Needs to Know* (Boston: Houghton Mifflin, 1987); Neil Postman, *Amusing Ourselves to Death: Public Discourse in the Age of Show Business* (New York: Viking, 1985).

11. Jim Collins, *Architectures of Excess: Cultural Life in the Information Age* (New York: Routledge, 1995), p. 138.

12. Ibid., p. 139.

13. Umberto Eco, 'The city of robots', in Thomas Docherty (ed.), *Postmodernism: A Reader* (Brighton: Harvester Press, 1993), p. 202.

14. Kumar, *Utopias*, p. 73.

15. Stjepan G. Mestrovic, *The Coming Fin de Siècle: An Application of Durkheim's Sociology to Modernity and Post-modernism* (London: Routledge, 1991), p. 3.

16. See Karen B. Mann, 'Narrative entanglements: The Terminator', *Film Quarterly* 43, 2 (Winter 1989–90) pp. 17–27.

17. Stephen Jay Gould, *Wonderful Life: The Burgess Shale and the Nature of History* (London: Hutchinson Radius, 1989), pp. 283–91.

I want to thank Cerys Evans for sharing with me her insights into *Bill & Ted's Excellent Adventure*.

9

Robin Hood: Men in Tights: Fitting the Tradition Snugly

Stephen Knight

Written and produced by Mel Brooks in 1993, one more in his series of pantsdown pastiches, *Men in Tights* was hated by most reviewers. To the sensitive newspaper types, this travesty of outlaw nobility (whether fraternally British or just Warner Brothers) was so crass it made them cross. More surprisingly, the postmodernist pontificators of the marginal journals found it worse yet, the jokes being too broad for their narrow understanding of parodic transgression.

Perhaps there was also a famine of Robin Hood scholarship. Well it's time to tuck in; or to Friar Tuck in. Or to Rabbi Tuchman in, to refer to one of Brooks's characteristic moments of irreverence.[1] Actually, having just written a paper on the outlaw in Scotland called 'Rabbie Hood' I thought of calling this one 'Rabbi Hood', but let it pass.

My purpose here is to respond to the trashing that Brooks's film received by arguing that it is in fact in the mainstream of the Robin Hood tradition, or one of them. When you excavate the Robin Hood materials as I have recently done[2] you find that comedy, parody, transgression and farce are intimate and dynamic parts of the whole from the beginning to the present. This is a popular myth in many ways, including in its vulgar forms.

There are many strands running through the Robin Hood tradition which are *not* woven into *Men in Tights* – social conflict, gentrification, heritage, nationalism, romantic individualism and many another ism and schism. Three strands which are relevant to this film, and which recur through the whole five hundred and more years of the recorded myth, are: borrowing with change, local reference, and comic transgression. In *Men in Tights* the third of these, comic transgression, is clearly the master code and pervades the other two, but there is nothing unusual in one theme dominating and directing the others – as in the stodgy liberalism of the Kevin Costner film (1991) and in the not unrelated tub-thumping nationalism of Scott's *Ivanhoe*: in both cases local reference dominates and directs the structure of borrowing with change. To give some instances of these three strands through the tradition, before looking at the film in these terms, it might be helpful to fix just what they can encompass and also to show how the first two, more obviously theme-oriented, can in earlier formations also be imbued with transgressive comedy.

A typical strand of borrowing with change can be traced by focusing, for once, on Marian, and this also often illustrates the burlesque features of the tradition. Marian, Robin Hood's partner, doesn't appear in the earliest ballads. Basically she emerges when the rough-handed social bandit of those texts is transmuted into a displaced gentleman; being a lord, he needs a lady, so he can leave his land to someone. The name Marion appears to come in part from the morris dance tradition, and may originally in this genre mean the 'Maurean' or the black one, but it is condensed with the Marion figure from medieval French romantic songs featuring Robin et Marion.

Yet the woman appears first in the Robin Hood legend in a decidedly unladylike form when, in a short play version of the conflict between Robin and the Friar,[3] it is the holy man who gets the girl. And what a girl:

She is a trull of trust
To serve a friar at his lust,
A prycker, a prauncer, a tearer of sheetes,
A wagger of ballockes when other men slepes.

It is not clear if the active party in the last two lines is this proto-Marion or the friar; one text turns 'A wagger of ballockes' into 'A wagger of buttockes', but is this a euphemism or simply a masculinisation of the action?

Perhaps it is just as well that Mel Brooks's research didn't go this far. His Marian is more closely related to the ladylike heroine brought forward in Anthony Munday's two plays, the *Downfall* and *Death* of Robin Hood, which appeared in

1598–99. Here she is really Lady Matilda Fitzwater (a solidly Norman name) who becomes Marian in her forest exile, just as the Earl of Huntingdon became Robin Hood. Even here though she experienced transgression: in the ballad where her story is told, she flees to the forest in disguise, meets a fierce outlaw who insists on fighting with this personable young gentleman until: 'The blood ran apace from Bold Robin's face / And Marian was wounded sore'.[4] They make friends of course, as Robin does with his other sparring partners. They are identified as a couple, but as lord and lady, not like Friar and girlfriend. Location conditions reference: this is a gentrified context, a pastoral world where passion does not run. That absence of overt emotive discourse was, as historians of the family and affect have argued, an acculturated form of local reference, and it changes as the locale ideologically alters.

A higher level of affect gathers around Robin and Marian in later versions, and these romanticising changes occur within a framework of borrowing both from the tradition and other sources. Diane Elam has argued in *Romancing the Postmodern*[5] that it is on the basis of the open structure of romance, to her inherently a non-realistic and so postmodern form, that myths of history, in all their factitious certainty can be constructed. This is a vertiginous argument, and this is not the place to try the handholds, but Elam has a clear place and time in mind. However, it is certainly intriguing to note that it is just as Scott and then Peacock locate the Robin Hood story in the domain of history and nationalism that romantic notions such as passion, jealousy and pro-active love enter the tradition. Ivanhoe has to choose between the socially (genetically?) important Saxon princess Rowena and the personally magnetic Jewess Rebecca. As the Robin Hood tradition develops along these emotively conflicted lines of identity and romance, it is the diabolically handsome sheriff who entraps, and threatens to entrance, Robin's female other. The triangle structure has played an especially strong role in American popular culture, from Reginald de Koven's musical version in the late nineteenth century on, and it is vigorously alive today, including, in comic mode, *Men in Tights*.

Brooks's version of Marian is basically a bedroom Barbie, and this has its own filmic sources as I will shortly suggest. But the modern period has also constructed, in radically changeful borrowing, the outlaw woman as an exact opposite to the triangular receptor, in the fiercely sleeves-rolled-up hero (for so she is) of BBC television's series *Maid Marian*, best described as feminist farce. Here Robin is a less than macho costume-designer and his one-time frail beloved, vividly and vigorously played by Kate Lonergan, has to train the burlesque guerrillas.

Ideological relocation works in those ways to renovate the tradition transgressively. It can have large forms, as above, or lower and more specific versions. An 1846 pantomime identified the sheriff as a spec builder who was, as was indeed then the case, covering Sherwood with little brick houses. Location can also be ideological: Martin Parker in 1632 placed the narrative firmly in the discourse of protestantism, making Robin's true heroism his resistance against a corrupt church; and it can be historical as with the anti-Nazi nuances of Michael Curtiz's 1938 film starring Errol Flynn.

As for burlesque transgression through the tradition, a couple of ripe instances should give the flavour and make the film seem quite traditional. After the success of Munday's Robin Hood plays, his company, the Admiral's Men, seem to have set out on a voyage of intoxicated discovery in the myth, and produced the highly intricate disguise comedy *Looke Aboute You* in 1600.[6] This seems to have been the product of all the company's writers working together, and drinking together too to judge by the zany plot, and especially by my favourite stage direction: '*Enter Robin Hood in the Lady Fauken-bridge's gowne, night attire on his hed*'. Little John was too big for that sort of cross-dressing, but not for his own form of burlesque. In one of the eighteenth-century Robin Hood musicals John becomes entangled with the wife of the Pindar of Wakefield. But the Pindar comes home, so John hides under the bed disguised as Towzer the dog, and is then given scraps to eat by the cuckolded but pet-loving husband – it's a piece of classic comic business. The Pindar leaves, and John is back at it, but then hubbie of course returns again, and this time John is hidden in the cradle, to be well kissed by the affectionate father. The sequence ultimately comes from the ancient Wakefield Second Shepherd's Play's parody of the birth of Jesus and both are in the fine tradition of transgressive farce that, like borrowing with change and local reference, are all part of the traditional quality of *Men in Tights*.

Analysis of the film itself finds a substantial amount of borrowing with change, with references to most of the recent film versions of the tradition and also less elaborate but still significant elements of local reference, and pure transgressive burlesque. Let's look at the details.

Especially in its opening sequences, *Robin Hood: Men in Tights* refers frequently to recent films in the outlaw tradition. The precredit sequence has fire arrows flying in improbable numbers across the screen, so burlesquing the 'mourning the dead' sequence at the end of 'The Sorcerer' episode of Harlech TV's *Robin of Sherwood* (1984), crossed with the trick shots of arrows used in Morgan Creek's *Robin Hood: Prince of Thieves* (1991). In this opening sequence the villagers complain about the regularity with which film companies burn their village, and so a mocking finger is pointed at the first episode of *Robin of Sherwood*, a Vietnam-inspired piece of Norman brutality. When a black rapper and supporting group talk us into the story, Brooks refers to the droll opening to the BBC's *Maid Marian* (1988) given by Danny John Jules as Barrington, a Rastafarian Allan a Dale; and then the escape from an Arab prison with a powerful African-American called Asneeze makes legitimate fun of the opening of *Prince of Thieves* where Costner's Robin is supported by a real black Moslem.

Minor references abound: in the opening the hands-through-the-grill shot mocks a similar but melodramatically sombre sequence in *Robin of Sherwood*. More pervasively, Cary Elwes, in his diminutive fashion, has an accent, costume and habit of beard-stroking very like that borne more grandly by Errol Flynn in *The Adventures of Robin Hood*, directed by Michael Curtiz in 1938. Another link to that landmark production comes when the Normans, after Robin arrives in England, beat his new friend, Achoo, son of Asneeze, much as they attacked Much in Curtiz's version.

The sightless servant who sits in the lavatory of Robin's ancestral hall reading a braille *Playboy* is a grotesque version of the highly sentimentalised ancient blind retainer in Costner's film, while Roger Rees continues that connection with his replay of Alan Rickman's barnstorming villain as the Sheriff of

Rottingham. Geraldine McEwen's somewhat threatening witch from the 1991 film is here transmogrified for laughs by Tracy Ullman as the lust-crazed loathly lady Latrine – she has changed her name from Shithouse, no doubt a nod to the old Jewish gag about the man who changed his name from Levy to Cohen because it was more respectable.

The 1938 film is obviously referred to when Brooks's tiny Robin staggers into the hall carrying a pig, of all things (Flynn swaggered in bearing a stag). Then there is a ludicrous version of the fight on the bridge where Robin and John keep breaking their staffs and end up at a catscradle level of conflict. The famous fencing encounter between Flynn and Sheriff Rathbone is replayed by Elwes and Rees, introduced with the mode-transgressive announcement, 'prepare for the fight scene', and featuring a version of the original fighting shadows on the wall, which they turn to a farcical game of shadow play with finger-modelled rabbit and duck.

Flynn and friends are not the only celluloid nobility to be invoked. The appearance of the grandly Scottish Patrick Stewart (from the later versions of *Star Trek*) as King Richard naturally refers to Sean Connery's sudden unveiling as the returning king in Costner's version (which itself had links with Jason Connery's appearance as Robert, Earl of Huntington, in the second sequence of *Robin of Sherwood*, not to mention Sean's starring role as the outlaw in *Robin and Marion*, 1976, in a sort of filial filiation).

This all indicates that Brooks and his advisers had looked carefully at the recent Robin Hood movies and television – but not, it would seem, at the other 1991 film starring Patrick Bergin and Uma Thurman – though in its rather politicised account of the myth, it might have been judged less burlesquable. However a much less well known Robin Hood film is clearly a partial source for *Men in Tights*. In 1984 there appeared *The Zany Adventures of Robin Hood* (from the team who made *Love at First Bite*) starring George Segal in distinctly baggy green tights as an earnest, timid and often puzzled version of the outlaw hero. Most spectacularly it starred Morgan Fairchild as a distinctly randy Marian – 'I'll soon be Old Maid Marian' she cried with feeling – and the chastity belt equipped cutie of *Men in Tights*, played by Amy Yasbeck, is clearly a low voltage version of this formidable figure. In the same way, the final joke of hero and heroine being married by one Rabbi Tuchman – whom Brooks fully equipped with dreadlocks and circumcising gear – links with the 1984 film's wonderfully bizarre sequence in which, Marian being imprisoned as usual, Robin goes to a friend to borrow money for bribery. It is no one but Isaac of York, from Scott's *Ivanhoe*, who (in the excitable person of Kenneth Griffith acting his head off) regrets his poverty but recommends some friends: Robin enters the castle with a team of Israeli commandoes, who perform the rescue, mutter 'Shalom' and steal off into the dark. By comparison with this farrago of Jewish referentiality, Brooks's appearance as Tuchman, like the sweet frustrations of Yasbeck's Marian, is simply modest fun.

If the film is in these ways deeply indebted to aspects of the recent Robin Hood tradition, strongly exemplifying the mainstream function of borrowing with change, it also exhibits richly a form of localisation.

Several of the changes already described point in a Hollywood direction – the Jewish humour and the Morgan Fairchild material, for instance. Then there's the naming of Will Scarlett O'Hara, as well as the guying of other Robin Hood films as in the tiny imitation of Flynn, the shadow-play scene and the assertion that this Robin at least can (unlike Costner) speak with an English accent. Stronger reference to the frenetic Californian world is found in the representation of Prince John by Richard Lewis as a flamboyant but cowardly type, a producer to the life, in the Hollywood musical assemblage of the villagers and outlaws on several occasions, and the especially farcical scene where Robin sings to, or rather at, Marian with all the heavy-handedness of a Mario Lanza tonsil opera: her hair-do is desperately windblown by his powerful top notes.

Other stray localisations are the imitation of *Home Alone* when the small (and not uncostneresque) boy at the beginning is pursued by the Normans,[7] and the sideswipe at those who managed to join the National Guard rather than go on Crusade. But finally this sort of Hollywood localisation verges over into the third of the mainstream strands in this film, when at the archery contest Robin loses – or appears to, when his opponent splits Robin's arrow. Stung by this surprising event, Robin, and then all the other major players, pull out the script and discover he really wins. The hero brings together referentiality, localisation and transgression by firing from his bow a Patriot Arrow straight from the Gulf War which does the generically rectifying trick.

Self-conscious burlesque is the essence of comic transgressiveness and it runs right through the film. Robin's early entry to the Arab dungeon is supervised by a Brown Derby style Maitre de Dungeon called Felafel; Robin is tortured with a grotesquely elastic piece of tongue pulling; as they escape the camels bear racetrack numbers; Achoo has the latest pump shoes; Locksley Hall is being trundled off on home-moving rollers as a result of a repossession; there is a parking lock on a horse; Robin's speech to the people (very much a la Flynn) ends up promising to protect the forests and ensure affordable health care. Towards the end this level of transgressive comedy and even brainless fun becomes more and more a matter of good old theatrical reliables: they send a 'fax' strapped to the side of (in a broad American accent) a fox. Simpler yet, there is much laughter, a good few minutes of mugging, when the Sheriff's first name is revealed at his wished-for marriage to Marian, as 'Mervyn'; the hangman, after the foiled execution, receives back the arrow-cut hangman's noose with the execrable joke 'No noose is good noose.' The final moment of this grotesque level of childish fun is when Robin, feeling he has defeated his victim in a final fight scene obviously lifted from the Costner film, smartly slaps his sword under his arm and in so doing effortlessly spits the sheriff, creeping up behind with a typically treacherous dagger.

All ends in farce, reference, harmless and tasteless fun, and so the film resolves itself fully in one of the many mainstream modes of the Robin Hood tradition, a tradition so powerful that it encloses, as in any trickster-based genre, its own empowering element of trash and self-trashing.

The theatricality and referentiality, the ultimately banal, familiar, pre and postmodern vitality of the whole performance is well conveyed in the sequence when Robin sings to Marian. By accident they are behind a white sheet. On the other side gather the outlaws, quite a large audience in this greenwood picture show, like any body of easily entertained and excitable folk, ourselves to the life. However, they think they see a very different story in shadow, as Robin's sword, while he leans back for the high notes, erects itself from the level of his groin to an angle well above horizontal.

The moment is potent. Like Brooks's whole version of the Robin Hood tradition, it is only teasing, and yet there is a promise and an avowal in the shadow play of an exciting form of jouissance. In this cinematic foreplay we sense the thrust of a myth whose traditional vitality is in part embodied in its power to be trashed, that is referentially, relocationally, transgressively mocked. And so re-created.

Notes

1. Acknowledgements to Seymour Chatman for confirming that Robin Hood was a topic of one of Brooks's parody scripts for the Sid Caesar show; he also offered the tail-note that 'Tuch' in Yiddish means 'ass' or, in Britain, 'arse'.
2. See *Robin Hood: A Complete Study of the English Outlaw* (Oxford: Blackwell, 1994).
3. Printed at the end of the *Gest of Robin Hood* in William Copland's edition, *c.*1560; for a text see R.B. Dobson and Taylor, *Rymes of Robin Hood* (London: Heinemann, 1976), pp. 208–14.
4. See 'Robin Hood and Maid Marian', in F.J. Child, *The English and Scottish Popular Ballads*, reprint ed. (New York: Dover), vol. III, pp. 218–19.
5. Diane Elam, *Romancing the Postmodern* (London: Routledge, 1993); this discussion is conducted through the Introduction, pp. 1–19 and Ch. 2, 'Walter Scott and the progress of romance', pp. 51–79.
6. Anthony Munday, *Looke Aboute You* (London: Ferbrand, 1600; reprinted London: Malone Society, 1913).
7. An acknowledgement to David Knight, youthful researcher, for this reference.

10

Pulpmodernism: Tarantino's Affirmative Action

Peter and Will Brooker

No one can doubt that Tarantino and his works are a cult. Over two thousand disappointed British Film Institute members applied in advance for the 616 tickets (including overspill) available for his personal appearance and a showing of his favourite film *Rio Bravo* at the National Film Theatre at the end of January 1995. The box office reported up to four hundred calls a day up to the Saturday of his visit; hundreds queued for stand-bys, and touts were selling tickets at four times their original price.[1]

The Tarantino phenomenon is of course inspired, somewhat uniquely, by more than his own two directed films. Other films with which he is associated include *True Romance* (screenplay), *Natural Born Killers* (screenplay) and *Killing Zoe* (associate producer). The published screenplays and soundtracks of *Reservoir Dogs* and *Pulp Fiction* have reached unprecedented sales for this kind of publication. The *Pulp Fiction* screenplay topped the 1994 pre-Christmas lists in the UK and at the time of writing the soundtrack is at no. 4 in the albums chart. As Mark Kermode points out, thanks to the soundtrack album, many fans 'would have known whole speeches *before* they even saw the film'.[2] This kind of exponential popularity is only further spiced by the fact that Oliver Stone managed to temporarily block the publication of the screenplay of *Natural Born Killers* and that *Reservoir Dogs* was refused video certification for a year. *Pulp Fiction* renewed interest in *Reservoir Dogs* and in the other spin-offs, boosting Tarantino's reputation as writer, producer, sometime actor and populist man about cinema for our fractured, non-hierarchical times ('To be elitist about the film industry is a cancer', he has said).[3] His picture is everywhere, a portrait of the artist as young fan, the defender of popular American cinema (who cites *Rio Bravo* and Sylvester Stallone rather than *High Noon* or Anthony Hopkins), the smart kid and one-time videoshop salesman who's made it, the slacker as *auteur*.

Much of this is reported with no more than the amused eye of the bystander used to the passing fame and spectacle expected of the postmodern. Tarantino's films themselves meanwhile have been both much praised and a cause of concern and controversy. James Wood, for example, has seen his 'brilliant' films as symptoms of our *fin de siècle* 'hectic postmodern', a period of 'trivial' and 'vacant' mass media and of a 'vaguely prurient' interest in increasing violence. Tarantino captures all this, says Wood, but is its trapped victim.[4]

Wood's comments are themselves symptomatic of a reaction to the postmodern and postmodernism whose 'final triumph', as represented by Tarantino, he says, 'is to empty the artwork of all content, thus voiding its capacity to do anything except helplessly *represent* our agonies (rather than to contain or comprehend)'.[5] In the same vein Fintan O'Toole would place Tarantino's films as 'Exhibit A in the museum of postmodern moral vacuity'. His brilliance, O'Toole thinks, shines less in his film-making than in his clever exploitation of the jaded appetites of the mass culture market. What he has 'done with violence' is pornographic since it appears on screen without even the rudimentary trappings of sequential plot or any pretence 'that his characters are more than stock borrowings from old movies'. He ' has disavowed all moral or social intent and gone straight for the sadism'.[6] Both critics speak out against postmodernism in the name of a beleaguered humanism and organicist aesthetic (Wood's notion in particular of art's function being to contain or comprehend our agonies echoes down a long tradition, most famously associated with Matthew Arnold). Not surprisingly this perspective requires its bad twin to sustain it. This these critics find in Tarantino and post-modernism, or what we have to say is a version of postmodernism (Wood invokes a second expression of the postmodern, though he recruits this to his own view, in comparing Tarantino to Don DeLillo). This same perspective is adopted by, amongst others, Mark Kermode, though for an apparently opposite purpose. Tarantino's work is referenced to other films, Kermode has said; it is film about film, 'the entertainment value of watching it is entirely cinematic'.[7] Kermode offers this as a defence of the film's merits. We might think that this view therefore refutes Wood and O'Toole's arguments but it does not, for it is fundamentally to see the film in the same way: as empty of social and moral content. In a fuller and more explicit reading which reveals how compatible these views in fact are, Amanda Lipman detects a series of warped repeats of several actors' earlier roles in what she terms 'this rag bag of film references'.[8] Thus Bruce Willis is seen to play a version of his *Die Hard* persona, Rosanna Arquette might be her character in *After Hours*, Harvey Keitel stages a domesticated reprise of his role 'in the *Nikita* remake *The Assassin*' and John Travolta is the street boy dancer Tony Manero of *Saturday Night Fever* a few years on and a few pounds heavier. If Tarantino has anything to say in all this, Lipman concludes, it is that 'there is no morality or justice in the patterns of life or death. Instead, the nihilist argument continues, there is trivia.'[9]

If we seek neither to celebrate nor judge the film in these terms but to understand it in relation to contemporary artistic and social trends, the issue that current discussion puts before us is that of 'violence', or the rights and wrongs of a supposed new 'aesthetic of violence' (stretching from Sarah Kane's *Blasted* to Eric Cantona's temper). Manhola Dargis pigeonholed *Pulp Fiction* six months before its release as another 'bone-shattering, skin-splitting, blood spurting' contribution to Tarantino's 'cinema of viscera ... written on the flesh of outlaw men and women.'[10] Violence is Tarantino's 'watchword', Amanda Lipman agrees, but what he says with it is that 'Life in the 90s ... is speedy and worthless'.[11] In Kermode's view, Tarantino's work is 'so postmodern' that the portrayal of violence 'doesn't mean anything'.[12]

What, in this light, can be said if we ask less about this art's forms (which are of concern to both Wood and Kermode) than its function: who is it for and what does it do? One reply is that Tarantino's fans are young males bereft of role models needing some guidance in how to get by in a violent world. Yet some significant social facts, as well as the aesthetic experience of the film, contradict or at least qualify this, contextualising its moments of violence in a different way. The *Guardian*, for example, reported that the London National Film Theatre audience was 'a cross section of age and gender'.[13] Beyond this metropolitan audience it's a fair guess (if only a guess) that the bulk of fans – who tend to miss events in the capital – are students, both male and female. (In courses taught by the authors two women and one man have volunteered class presentations on Tarantino.) Arguably, violence is an issue for these fans because it has been made one by the media. And if we say, rightly, that violence is nonetheless a real contemporary social issue we should note that, aside from the issues of class and social division it entails, this concern has brought a new critical attention to violence by women and to its cultural representation as well as to violent acts by men.[14]

If we are going to understand the relevance to this issue of Tarantino's work, it is unhelpful, not to say crass, to associate his films and postmodernism in an undifferentiated way with the amoral, superficial and self-referential portrayal of violence. We are concerned mainly here with *Pulp Fiction* but it is clear that the tone and nature of violence in this film is different from the previous *Reservoir Dogs* (both of which ought in turn to be distinguished from *Killing Zoe* and *Natural Born Killers*). The torture scene in *Reservoir Dogs* presents a different mode of violence to the careless shooting of Marvin, to cite the most obviously violent scene in the second film. It would be surprising if these scenes did not provoke a different reaction or serve a different possible 'social function', just as they function differently in the film's internal worlds. More to the point, however, what viewers respond to most immediately in *Pulp Fiction* are the dialogue and the monologues these often harbour, and above all scenes like the opening car ride, Vincent's dance at Jackrabbit Slim's 50s retro restaurant and the Wolf's clean-up campaign at Jimmie's house. These scenes are not about violence but about relationships and about style. In their dress, speech and manner, the characters display an attitude, in its fullest sense, of cool eccentricity. And again although the male characters are attractive and comic in this way to both male and female audiences, so too are Mia Wallace (Uma Thurman) and a minor character such as Jody (played by Rosanna Arquette).

We have to think beyond a traditional humanist aesthetic and more broadly than an 'aesthetic of violence' if we are to account for these features and for this kind of pleasure. We have, that is to say, to think with more discrimination and subtlety about the aesthetic forms and accents of postmodernism – so famously 'all about style' but not by that token always only about 'merely' style. *Pulp Fiction*'s postmodernism does not produce a *hermetic* self-mirroring intertextualism nor administer *only* to male narcissism and a subordinated female gaze (which are less constraining than film theory sometimes likes to believe). Nor do we have to deny the film's self-knowingness (and the audience's pleasure in this and their own) to argue that it relates to moral issues and how to live rather than kill and die. We want to show that *Pulp Fiction* in particular, though importantly not in isolation, is more affirmative, less vacuous and nihilistic than critics like Wood and O'Toole believe and less self-enclosed than Kermode accepts; that in keeping with its own revaluative inflection of a postmodern aesthetic it offers a 'life-style' – otherwise so cheap a phrase of the end of century – which redeems and recasts the pulp of the postmodern in the very style and structure of its fictional narrative. To appreciate this we need to return firstly to the question of the film's cult status and secondly to consider its relation to the more familiar features of postmodernism.

Umberto Eco presents Michael Curtiz's *Casablanca* (1942) as an exemplary case of the cult film.[15] 'A cult movie is proof', he says, 'that, as literature comes from literature, cinema comes from the cinema' (p. 447). The cult film is characterised by an improvised, intertextual collage of stereotypical situations, or 'intertextual archetypes', already logged in the encyclopedia of cinema narrative, which when once again recycled, provoke an 'intense emotion' of recognition and the desire for repetition. But this repetition and the expression of affection for the film takes a particular form. 'A perfect movie', says Eco, 'remains in our memory as a whole' (p. 447). The cult movie, on the other hand, is imperfect, dislocated and 'unhinged ... It must live on, and because of, its glorious ricketiness' (p. 447). The fan will therefore recall discontinuous, selected images, or characters or snatches of dialogue, quoting 'characters and episodes as if they were aspects of the fan's private sectarian world, a world about which one can make up quizzes and play trivia games so that the adepts of the sect recognise through each other a shared expertise' (p. 446). This experience, Eco suggests, is culturally specific: the archetypes are 'particularly appealing to a given cultural area or a historical period' (p. 448). Rather than pursue the kind of social or cultural semiotics this would argue is appropriate to the film, however, Eco proceeds to offer a formalist and abbreviated thematic analysis, shot by shot, of the first twenty minutes of *Casablanca*. His entire discussion, moreover, is very clearly shadowed by a traditional aesthetic. Thus the cult is ramshackle and imperfect, it has no 'central idea or emotion' or 'coherent philosophy of composition' (p. 449). The cult movie, indeed works 'in defiance of any aesthetic theory'; it is primitive archetype, anonymous live textuality, 'outside the conscious control of its creators' (p. 447). 'Nature', he concludes, 'has spoken in place of men' (p. 454). Though he sees a sublimity in this self-perpetuating creation, it is clear that in the scale of aesthetic values Eco assumes the truly venerated terms are all on the other side of the cult film – and are much the same as those invoked by Wood and O'Toole. On this reckoning, the cult film can only be identified as the opposite of the authentic work of art understood as the conscious, coherent creation of the individual artist who 'tames' the raw matter of cultural cliché in the name of beauty and civilisation. In the postmodern film (Eco cites *Bananas*, *Raiders of the Lost Ark* and *ET*) the intertextuality which characterises the cult movie becomes predictably more self-conscious, for now both film-maker and viewer are 'instinctive semioticians' (p. 454): a development that Eco presents with a nostalgia for what perversely appears as the innocence of the original cult film, or cult of cult films which is *Casablanca*.

Certainly *Pulp Fiction* conforms to much in Eco's description. The film's status is confirmed and re-confirmed by the mere citation of a favourite cameo role or sequence, the imitation of a look or action (the dance, the costume of black suit, white shirt, straight tie carried over from *Reservoir Dogs*), by a quoted passage of dialogue and above all by the repetition, the echoing back to the film, of individual lines and phrases ('Royale with cheese' matching Bogart's 'Here's looking at you kid' or 'Play it again Sam'). Tarantino's admirers might not all be fans, of course, and not all fans will be cult fans. It is likely, however, that all viewers will be aware to some degree of the text or intertexts of its world of internal and ongoing reference. The rituals of repetition or mirroring, a saying back to the film and other fans, can be a way of expressing common or popular knowledge, or of displaying exceptionally detailed or new knowledge (culled, say, from a bootleg video or out-of-the-way interview). A fan's response will be affirming and self-affirming rather than questioning or analytical, more reflexive than reflective, but if this self-generating world (producing fan upon fan, cinema from cinema) can be trivial, pedantic and exclusive, it is not thereby finally confining nor isolating. Rather the reverse. Eco points to this double life of fandom in referring to the fan's 'private sectarian world' and 'shared expertise' above. There can be no solitary fan of the cult film. A cult enthusiasm is at once exclusive and shared, a socially expressed aesthetic built upon a fundamentally social emotion and experience.

The social form engendered by Tarantino's work, which helps counter the emphasis on the film's portrayal of violence as its main social content, is that of the group. According to Tarantino, before signing up for *Pulp Fiction*, Bruce Willis and his brothers would spend afternoons at home 'riffing on scenes from *Dogs*' – 'like old buddies', Mark Kermode adds, 'enjoying a communal singalong'.[16] Kermode talks, without further comment, of the suitability of the speeches on the *Pulp Fiction* soundtrack for 'drunken rendition'.[17] If this is indeed the social form fandom takes, we have some reason for thinking of its pleasures as predominantly and stereotypically 'male'. Even so, however adolescent and boorish we might find this front-room camaraderie, it is not of itself violent – any more than pub or football terrace culture are – nor amoral.

The cult world of the films also has a quite different potential, however, once again both paradoxically internalised and expanding. For the hard-core fan Tarantino as *auteur* has created an entire world of cross-references across not two but in the first instance at least four films. Thus Vince Vega is traceable as cousin, or brother, to Vic 'Mr Blonde' Vega in *Reservoir Dogs*, while Vic's parole officer, Scagnetti, is a central character in

Natural Born Killers. Mr White's reference to his old flame Alabama leads us back to *True Romance*, while a scene cut from the completed film reveals that the nurse who Nice Guy Eddie was going to fetch for the mortally-wounded Orange is Bonnie, Jimmie's wife from *Pulp Fiction*. The path of this cross-referencing leads us to identify Mr Brown/Tarantino and Jimmie/Tarantino as one and the same man. This is the boys-own stuff of the Internet possibly, but it is only a film's width away from the erudition of literary scholarship, from learned revelations on the modernist classics or poststructuralist readings of a story by Edgar Allan Poe. That this is an active, producerly reading of the Tarantino texts would be hard to deny. It is in the nature of intertextuality also that it extends itself, across film texts and popular media in this case, to the music of the 1950s and 1960s on the film soundtracks, to the stories of *Black Mask* magazine, the crime writer Charles Willeford who Tarantino alludes to, to Ralph Meeker in *Kiss Me Deadly*, to Aldo Ray in Jacques Tourneur's *Nightfall* (a role he and Willis agreed on as a model for Butch in *Pulp Fiction*), to the films of Roger Corman and Howard Hawkes, and to the selections from American and European cinema he has introduced in a programme of films at the National Film Theatre.

If this appears to threaten a relation of pied-piping movie sage to cloned disciples, winding their way down the endless by-ways of pulp (would a true fan pause to check out all the Roger Corman films pictured on the posters in Jackrabbit Slim's?), we might remember the nature of the dispute, as Tarantino sees it, between himself and Oliver Stone. 'He wants every single one of you to walk out thinking like he does. I don't. I made *Pulp Fiction* to be entertaining. I always hope that if one million people see my movie, they saw a million different movies.'[18] This unfettered libertarianism goes hand in hand with an expanding intertextuality and contrasts not only with the closed world the term 'cult' at first suggests but with the aesthetic ideal of containment and the comprehension of our agonies assumed by Wood above. Both ideas of art's function are didactic and both, contrary again to Wood's belief, have a moral aspect.

The romantic humanist aesthetic that Wood, O'Toole and Eco espouse has long been questioned within modernism and contemporary theory alert to the key significance of the fragment, the internally contradictory, and the marginal. The deconstructive effect of an intertextual postmodernism is precisely to challenge distinctions between the original and authentic and true, the unified, high and centred on the one hand and the copy, the false, the low, the supplementary and marginal on the other. The problem with a traditional aesthetic lies not so much in the position itself, however, as the nostalgia and presumption with which it is held, leading these and other writers to simplify and so patronise or dismiss the challenge of postmodernism. To see this tendency in contemporary culture as no more than a nihilistic indulgence in clever-clever bricolage, a provocative but unfeeling cultivation of excess, is to take a commentator like Jean Baudrillard and declarations on the contemporary loss of the real and any ethical perpective at their word. There are more testing questions to ask about postmodernism's oppositional, critical and liberating aspect and its relation to a social and cultural past and future, and there are quite obvious distinctions also between kinds of postmodernism, or accents within the range of cultural expression the term encompasses. If some examples of postmodern art are at once scandalous and vacant, or 'merely' playful, others are innovative and deeply problematising. If some are symptomatic, others are exploratory. Like postmodern society, cultural postmodernism is various and contradictory: fatalistic, introverted, open, inventive, and enlivening. *Pulp Fiction* visits these contradictions and requires a fuller, dialectical reading if we are to appreciate its own double aspect.

Much that has been said above of the film's intertextuality might be glossed by reference to what now pass as the leading features of postmodernism: its pastiche, self-imitation, loss of affect, loss of historical sense, loss of social reference and hence critical or affirmative influence. This is the stuff of the charges brought against the film above. Unquestionably, *Pulp Fiction* echoes and alludes to other films (most conspicuously to Godard's *Bande A Part* for the dance scene in Jackrabbit Slim's). It has no specific location nor setting in time. If the reference to McDonald's and Burger King in Europe, Jody's body-piercing or Jules's cellular phone indicates a present time in the late 1980s or early 1990s, Vince's car is a '74 Chevy

Nova, the music belongs to the 1960s and 1970s, the TV references (to *Kung Fu*, *Happy Days*, and Mia's pilot *Fox Force Five* – both the latter already party to *le mode retro*) suggest the late 1970s, the dialogue on occasion ('daddy-o' and 'kooties') belongs to the 1950s or the 1950s recycled, and the movie-star look-alike waiters and waitresses of Jackrabbit Slim's itself to the no time/any time of echt postmodern period pastiche.

On this evidence we might indeed read the film as an amusing but pathological symptom of postmodern superficiality, unwitting proof of the randomised indifference of a thoroughly commercialised, magpie aesthetic, which blithely apes the supposed free flow of goods across the global markets of late capitalism. Yet at the same time *Pulp Fiction* displays some important contrary features. Those associated with its cult following and open, enlightening intertextuality we have already pointed to. Here we want to comment particularly on the film's episodic, circling narrative structure. This is once more a conspicuous, popularly noticed feature of the film (distinguishing it in composition and structure of feeling from *Reservoir Dogs* and other films associated with Tarantino, while suggesting a resemblance with, say, *Short Cuts* and a number of postmodern prose narratives) whose effects also have a significant bearing on the issue of violence.

The attitude towards narrative in postmodern theory is well-known, and conveniently summarised by Edward Said. Both Lyotard and Foucault, he says, have turned their attention away from the forces of radical opposition and insurgency to problem-solving games, local issues, and the 'microphysics of power' surrounding the individual:

> The self was therefore to be studied, cultivated, and, if necessary, refashioned and constituted. In both Lyotard and Foucault we find precisely the same trope employed to explain the disappointment in the politics of liberation: narrative which posits an enabling beginning point and a vindicating goal, is no longer adequate for plotting the human trajectory in society. There is nothing to look forward to: we are stuck within our circle.[19]

Circling mini-narratives do not have this necessary set of implications, however. In *Pulp Fiction*, two characters, first of all, Jules and Butch undergo or contrive a transformation in which they gain new purpose and a sense of 'long-term' direction. Jules believes he has been saved from death by divine intervention and sets to reinterpret the text of Ezekiel 25:17 (a fake quotation) which he customarily recites before a killing to new ends. If he has been the 'evil man' rather than the 'righteous man' of this text, striking down those 'who attempt to poison and destroy my brothers' in a parody of the vengeful agent of the Lord, he believes he can become the blessed man who 'shepherds the weak through the valley of darkness'. He forsakes a life of violent crime for the ancient grand narrative of 'charity and good will' ('I'm tryin', I'm tryin' real hard to be a shepherd' he says, and soon after in closing his criminal life does spare Pumpkin – 'Wanna know what I'm buyin', Ringo? Your life. I'm giving you that money so I don't hafta kill your ass'). For his part Butch backtracks on a narrative of pure self-preservation to save Marsellus from the humiliation of rape, and is able, with the 'blessing' of his enemy, to embark on the mythic narrative of a newly invented self, free of the 'violent' and crooked world of boxing.

Clearly these stories, and Butch's in particular, posit an ethical view of the world. Though it might require a transformative epiphany to realise its 'righteous' side, this ethical view is all the same consistent, on its 'bad' side, with the emphasis on partnership and group loyalty (a textual inspiration and reinforcement to some degree surely of fan loyalty) in both *Reservoir Dogs* and *Pulp Fiction*. This in turn is grounded in the disadvantaged circumstances of the male characters as working-class professional hoodlums (this shared class identity is strongly suggested in the opening scene of *Reservoir Dogs*, where Mr White argues the importance of tipping waitresses on a minimum wage). Lives of routine danger, the films tell us, require mutual support and a code of professional conduct if they are not to flare out of routine control. Jules insists in the first scene of *Pulp Fiction* that he and Vince 'get into character' before they make the hit. The hoods in *Reservoir Dogs* are bonded at the level of their abstract common identity. But the coded roles that marshall their actions are evidently narrow and brittle, tested by the undertow of quotidian dialogue they can barely squeeze out of the hitman's prescribed rhetoric, and broken by the crises the films' narratives unfold. Thus in *Reservoir Dogs* the blank, professional code deemed necessary to survival is transgressed by the pathological Mr Blonde and impersonated by Mr Orange. Real identities, bringing real friction and extreme violence, but also signs of a deeper comradeship, seep through their allotted anonymity and apparent sameness – as in the rapport that emerges between Mr White and Mr Orange. Both films explore the need for and fragility of fixed identities and relationships and do this analogically, through the use of stock generic characters such as 'the undercover cop', 'the hitman' and 'the boxer' and stereotypical scenarios such as 'the heist gone wrong', 'the hit', 'the crooked fight'. The films' characters are contained by or revert to these roles (Mr White, who has revealed himself as 'Larry', reverts to the relationship of cop and criminal once Mr Orange's duplicity is exposed). Or, on occasion, as in the examples of Jules and Butch, characters can redefine these roles and redirect their lives. Jules is finally neither 'the hitman', nor 'the bum' Vince says he will become: 'I'll just be Jules Vincent', he says, 'no more, no less.' Tarantino does not merely repeat nor pastiche the conventions of pulp cinema, therefore; he reinvents and extends these conventions, exposing their abstract 'cartoon' like rudiments, adding unexpected dialogue, a concentrated intensity or relaxed attenuation of plot or hyperbole of character. He gives them new life, we might say, just as Jules and Butch and Marsellus and Mia are granted new life and, at another level, the dipping, repetitive careers of actors such as Willis and Travolta are also revived.

One remarkable instance of this inventive and affirmative mode is perhaps worth particular comment and is of interest once more in relation to the topic of violence. Escorted home from the dance at Jackrabbit Slim's, Mia Wallace overdoses while Vince is in the bathroom. He races her to his dealers and plunges a syringe into her chest, guided by a handbook for such emergencies. His efforts save her life. Like the accidental killing of the black youth in Vince's car, this is a key scene in terms of the film's treatment of violence. Vince and Jules's reaction in this second case is callous in the extreme, but their combined indifference and heated bickering over the state of their clothes and of the car provoke a common audience reaction of dismay and disbelief, at their actions and the playing of the scene itself, rather than outrage. The moment edges scandalously towards slapstick and if we half suspect that their cold 'professionalism' is being parodied in this incident we know for sure that this is the intent of the following scene in which the Wolf cleans up the mess with military impersonality ('A please would be nice', Vince says huffily, as if to emphasise that common decency is not part of the Wolf's professional repertoire). Mia's 'resurrection', on the other hand, provokes a reaction of near hysterical relief. What is indeed disturbing rather than conformist about these scenes and helps re-channel stock reactions to the stock 'violence' underlying them is their mixed tone. Just as cinematic conventions are opened out, set in the fluctuating rhythms and distracting debris and dialogue of real life, so the conventions of viewing response are angled away from expectations. Scenes from the gangster genre, that is to say, are touched with unexpected comedy. Dan Glaister sees the image of 'a hypodermic needle plunged into the chest of an actress' as further evidence of Tarantino's graphic portrayal of violence,[20] when in fact this is the most graphic illustration of the film's theme of re-invention and rebirth. In plain terms, Mia is brought back from the dead. What is more, Vincent's life-saving stab decisively changes the tone of the film, to the point of unsettling its assumed generic base.

Tarantino's postmodernism therefore moves off from and against a fixed base, but not so as to become aimlessly decentred. No more is the narrative of *Pulp Fiction* pointlessly circling or enclosing. One thinks of Vincent Vega's dance at Jackrabbit Slim's – a controlled improvisation upon the standard form of the twist. And indeed the creative flexibility or accent which shapes the film's aesthetic and informs its ethical view is most strikingly developed in relation to this character. The 'long narratives' of hope and renewal associated with Jules and Butch strike off at a tangent from the film's main narrative movement. Vincent's fictional story, however, is entirely encompassed by it. Yet its effect, returning us to a scene before his death, is not to encircle or eliminate this character but to foreground and literally enliven him.

By implication the violence of Vince's death, and other acts of violence, are perceived as matters of fiction and not 'real' at all. This is what critics of postmodernism complain of, of course, seeking some effective relation of moral commentary between the two. But to be aware of fictionality does not entail a substitution of the unreal for the real so much as a realisation that the real is always constructed, its chronological plot always narrativised, our judgements upon it a matter of tone and perspective. In manipulating chronology, moreover, fiction can return us to better moments, as it does here in returning us to Vincent Vega in beach shirt and Bermudas with his buddy Jules, edgy but on top of his game, rather than the Vincent Vega who lies dead in a toilet, his white shirt blood-spattered because he was caught alone and off-guard. This episode also gives us our last glimpse of Marsellus Wallace, once more the untouchable gangster king and ordering in the Wolf on his poolside phone as if his rape had never happened; which of course, at this time, it has not. Creative memory (in an era that has lost a sense of the past) defies the deadly fate of conventional linear progression. Our perspective is once again angled away from the scene and sight of violence.

Vince is the only one of the four main characters to die rather than begin a new life. It is important, however, to see that this death is in a sense reasoned rather than arbitrary. In three significant moments Vincent retires to the bathroom (to talk himself into controlling the immediate future, to read the pulp novel *Modesty Blaise*). If these scenes function self-reflexively as an interlude to consult the narrative of *this* pulp fiction and its subsequent course, they gives Vince no effective guidance, since he returns to an utterly changed world where death is threatened (Mia's, as above; Jules and the others' in the cafe held up by Pumpkin and Honey Bunny) and where in the third instance he meets his own, shot by Butch with his own gun. Through Vince in particular we see the contemporary world as utterly contingent, transformed, disastrously, in the instant you are not looking. There is as they say a 'moral' here. Like Jules and Butch, Vince is given brief moments of reflection, when his story is effectively held on freeze-frame. When his narrative returns to speed, however, the world is changed around him and he adapts to it, but not in the gesture of radical self-revision that Jules and Butch bring to their equivalent moments of decision. The world of radical contingency requires a ready adjustment to the present composition and re-composition of events, a dialectical responsiveness (most decisively at a critical, life-threatening moment) that makes it possible to switch from the path of evil to the path of righteousness, to convert the fixed and routine into the original.

Perhaps after all Vince's dancing is too controlled, a set-piece without sufficient improvisation. The tension between stereotypes, from *Black Mask* and B movies, and the eccentric, transgressive variations upon them with which Tarantino invests plot and character determines the tragic outcome of *Reservoir Dogs* where Mr White must revert to type. Vince too dies as he lives, a hitman, and it is his personal tragedy that he does not exploit the moment of betweenness when in sidling out of the diner having saved the cafe, and granted Pumpkin his life, he is that hitman still but out of uniform, his gun stuck down his Bermuda shorts. Here in this moment too, he is significantly with his partner still. In a contingent world where anything might happen, including being blown away, the loner, slow to change, is surprised and lost.

But where Vince fails personally, the film's narrative does not fail him. If a fixed mode or code of conduct is ill-fitted to this world, so too is a linear narrative with beginning point, middle and end. The film's circling mini-narratives enable it to question the finality of this fated end, returning us to Vince's most potentially self-transformative moment in the diner (in which comedy serves again to unsettle the fixed type). In *this* end, the mosaic narrative movement of the film works miraculously to bring the dead Vincent Vega back to life, revived by Tarantino; not as in a sentimental reprise, but as if to start again, to consider from a new angle what might have been. (In the scene of the Hit we see from Marvin's point of view in the bathroom; in the diner Honey Bunny's dialogue re-commences after the earlier freeze-frame, and is heard differently by Jules.)

We should think then finally of an 'aesthetic of contingency' rather than of an 'aesthetic of violence'. While this describes a postmodern condition where 'anything can happen', including acts of extreme violence, it is not to endorse the undifferentiated 'anything goes' of a Baudrillardian postmodernism, or an indifference – with which the film is charged – to matters of life and death.

Tarantino's world is evidently saturated with enthusiasms, discriminations and declared preferences. It is full and affirmative rather than empty and nihilistic. His films have not sought to master, shape and control the contingent (the Wolf is the film's example of this traditional and high modernist ambition; now become, appropriately enough, mythological). Instead, both films and scripts select broadly and fluently from amongst cinematic motifs and cultural styles to assemble newly woven, open narratives which bring life to the dead, the has-been, the jaded, the banal. The past is recycled, its 'waste' products put to new creative advantage. The fixed and conventional are opened to new artistic and human connections. In this way *Pulp Fiction*, in particular, offers a *modus vivendi*: a way of telling, of living a postmodern narrative deeply embedded in world of narratives, which in giving new life to the familiar and conventional can spin out of the hermetic enclosure both of a narrowly defined genre fiction and a traditional fiction seeking a correspondence to 'reality'. The intertextual bricolage which makes avant-garde technique a popular pleasure is joined by an underlying, if frustrated, ethic of companionship; a surviving will to do another some good. This is the best that the best of modernism ever aimed for and the best perhaps that the humanism which takes such high-minded offence at the films can aspire to.

Yet Tarantino takes on more than either of these modes. For in making it new in the days of the postmodern, an affirmative popular art must reach lower, digging its way, eyes open, through the cultural strata to sample the mass and mess of pulp, the brutality of low and criminal life, and root it back up to the spreading generic surface of popular cinema entertainment.

Notes

1. *Independent on Sunday*, 27 January 1995, p. 2; *Guardian*, 30 January 1995, p. 22.
2. 'Endnotes', *Sight and Sound*, February 1995, p. 62.

3. *Guardian*, 30 January 1995.
4. *Guardian*, 19 November 1994, p. 31.
5. Ibid.
6. 'Bloody minded', *Guardian*, 3 February 1995, p. 16.
7. *The Late Show*, BBC2, 24 January 1995.
8. *Sight and Sound*, November 1994, p. 51.
9. Ibid.
10. *Sight and Sound*, May 1994, p. 6.
11. *Sight and Sound*, November 1994.
12. *The Late Show*, 24 January 1995. The panellists in this discussion, including Ros Coward and Stephen Daldry, were asked by Fintan O'Toole to address the question of an 'aesthetic of violence'.
13. *Guardian*, 30 January 1995, p. 22.
14. See, for example, Helen Birch (ed.), *Moving Targets: Women, Murder and Representation* (London: Virago, 1993) which includes discussion of the cases of Myra Hindley, the 'dingo baby murder', and Tracey Wigginton, and the films *Black Widow*, *Thelma and Louise* and *Fatal Attraction*. We might add the cases of Beverley Allitt and Rosemary West and the recent film *Heavenly Creatures*.
15. 'Casablanca: cult movies and intertextual collage', in *Travels in Hyperreality*, reprinted in David Lodge (ed.), *Modern Criticism and Theory* (London: Longman, 1988), pp. 446–55. Further page references are given in the text.
16. *Sight and Sound*, February 1995, p. 62.
17. Ibid.
18. *Guardian*, 30 January 1995, p. 22.
19. Edward Said, *Culture and Imperialism* (London: Chatto and Windus, 1993), p. 29.
20. *Sight and Sound*, May 1994, p. 6.

Index

actors
  reprise roles, 137
  signature on film, 35–6
Adventures of Robin Hood, 6–7,
  116, 128, 129, 130
aesthetic, romantic humanist,
  142–3
allusion, in *Bill & Ted*, 116
Ambridge, intertextual
  consumption of, 91
America, world consumerist
  culture of, 113, 121
Amis, Martin, 31
Anderson, Laurie, *Bright Red*
  album, 94
Arquette, Rosanna, in *Pulp
  Fiction*, 137, 138
audience
  and *Bill & Ted*, 115, 117
  mass, 87–8, 93–4
  for Tarantino films, 137–8
authenticity, of film
  adaptations, 11
author
  actor as, 35–6
  director as, 37–8
  and field of cultural
    production, 29
  and film adaptations, 3–4,
    100

Back to the Future, 115, 122
Bad Girls from Mars, 117–18
Bananas (film), 140
Barthes, Roland, 29, 74
Baudrillard, Jean, 143
Bazin, Andreé, 23, 28n
BBC TV costume drama, 85

Beethoven, in *Bill & Ted*, 119
Bell, Tom, in *The Magic
  Toyshop*, 103
Bergin, Patrick, *Robin Hood*
  (1991 film), 130
Bergman, Ingmar, 45
Bill & Ted's Bogus Journey
  (1991), 114, 116, 117, 122
Bill & Ted's Excellent Adventure,
  6, 7, 114–16
  historical parody in, 6,
    116–17, 119–20
  role of Rufus, 114, 118, 119,
    122, 123
Black Mask magazine, 142, 149
Blade Runner, 33, 120
(The) Bloody Chamber (Angela
  Carter's novel), 101,
  103–4
Bloom, Allan, relativism, 113,
  114
(The) Bonfire of the Vanities,
  14, 17
Bourdieu, Pierre, 3, 29, 30, 92
Branagh, Kenneth, 3, 5
  as actor, 67–8, 82n
  Beginnings (autobiography),
    77
  as director, 67
  gender imbalance in *Mary
    Shelley's Frankenstein*, 4,
    57–60, 68
  and *Henry V*, 77–8
  relationships with De Niro
    and Coppola, 63–4
Brooks, Mel, *Robin Hood: Men
  in Tights*, 7, 125, 129–31,
  133

153

camera, direct address to,
50–1, 52
Carter, Angela, 5–6
literary research on, 99
The Bloody Chamber, 99
and *The Company of Wolves*
(film), 103, 104–7
and *The Magic Toyshop*, 107
The Passion of New Eve, 102
The Sadeian Woman, 103
Wise Children, 102, 108
as writer, 100–1, 107–8
Casablanca, 139–41
class, and heritage industry,
92–4
classic literature, film
adaptations of, 2–3
Collick, John, on *Company of
Wolves*, 104, 106–7
Collins, Jim, on *Bill & Ted*,
115, 117
comic transgression, 128–9
in *Robin Hood: Men in
Tights*, 7, 125–6, 129–30
(*The*) *Company of Wolves* (film
adaptation of *Bloody
Chamber*), 103, 104–7
concretisation, of film
adaptations, 15–16, 17
Connery, Jason, in *Robin of
Sherwood*, 130
Connery, Sean, in *Robin Hood:
Prince of Thieves*, 130
consumer capitalism, triumph
of, 112
consumerism
of American culture, 113
and cultural nostalgia, 87–8
'heritage' souvenirs, 88–9
contingency, aesthetic of,
149–50
Cooper, Dennis, on Last Man,
112–13
Coppola, Francis Ford,
producer of *Mary Shelley's
Frankenstein*, 63–4

Corliss, Richard, review of *The
Bonfire of the Vanities*, 14
Corman, Roger, 142
Costner, Kevin, *Robin Hood:
Prince of Thieves*, 129, 131
Crisp, Quentin, in *Orlando*,
45, 49–50
Cruise, Tom, in *Interview with
the Vampire*, 33–5, 36–7
cult movies, 139–41
Bill & Ted, 114
Tarantino's, 135–6
cultural heritage
dissolution of common,
86–7
and education, 92–4
cultural production
academic relations to,
38–40
author and, 29, 30–1
large-scale, 30–1
postmodern, 2–3
restricted, 30, 31
culture, American
consumerist, 113, 121
Curtiz, Michael
Adventures of Robin Hood
(1938), 128, 129
Casablanca, 139

Dargis, Manhola, on *Pulp
Fiction*, 137
Darth Vader (*Star Wars*), 74,
76
Davies, Andrew, dramatisation of *Middlemarch*
(1994), 85
De Niro, Robert, in *Mary
Shelley's Frankenstein*,
62–4
De Palma, Brian, 14
de-differentiation
of cultural forms, 87, 88
of Middlemarch souvenirs,
89
Death, in *Bill & Ted*, 116, 117

Robin Hood
  early texts, 125–6, 127,
    128–9
  ideological relocations of,
    128
Robin and Marion (1976), 130
Robin of Sherwood (Harlech TV
    1984), 129
Robinson, David, on *Henry V*,
    76
RoboCop, 120
rock music, as universal
    culture in *Bill & Ted*, 121,
    122–3
Ross, Andrew, 38, 39

Sackville-West, Vita, 47, 48
Sage, Lorna, on Angela Carter,
    100
Said, Edward, 144
San Dimas, California,
    parodied in *Bill & Ted*,
    114, 119–20, 121, 122–3
science fiction, in *Bill & Ted*,
    115, 116, 120, 122–3
Scott, Gerry, designer for
    Middlemarch, 88
Scott, Sir Walter, *Ivanhoe*, 126,
    127
Scumbusters (1988 film), 117,
    118
Segal, George, as Robin Hood,
    130
Selznick, David O., 13–14
service industries, 93
(The) Seventh Seal (Bergman),
    116
sexuality, in Carter's work,
    99
Shakespeare, William
  Chorus in *Henry V*, 78
  National Curriculum and,
    79–80
Shelley, Mary, use of own
    story in Branagh's film,
    57–8, 66

Sherrin, Ned, in *Orlando*, 45
Shields, Rob, on
    consumption, 87–8
(The) Silence of the Lambs, 12
Sinfield, Alan (with
    Dollimore), on *Henry V*,
    75
Sluizer, George, *The Vanishing*,
    17, 19, 21, 22
Smith, John, curator of
    Stamford Museum, 90
Socrates, in *Bill & Ted*, 117,
    119
Sommerville, Jimmy, in
    Orlando, 45–6, 49
specificity (art-form), of film
    adaptations, 11
Stairway to Heaven, 116
Stamford
  choice of, 85–6
  increased tourism in, 92,
    93–4
  Middlemarch souvenirs,
    88–9, 90
  recreation of as
    Middlemarch, 88
  tourist confusion with
    Middlemarch, 89–91
Steiner, George, 121
Stewart, Patrick, in *Robin
    Hood: Men in Tights*, 130
Stone, Oliver, and Tarantino,
    135, 142
Swinton, Tilda, in *Orlando*, 43,
    49–50, 51

Tarantino, Quentin, 1, 2, 7–8
  Killing Zoe, 135
  Natural Born Killers
    (screenplay), 135
  Pulp Fiction, 135, 142, 150
  Reservoir Dogs, 135, 149
  Rio Bravo, 135, 136
  True Romance (screenplay),
    135
(The) Terminator movies, 122

Index by Auriol Griffith-Jones